Kr

Text by Sco
Edited by Alex Knights
Principal photographer: Gregory Wrona
Series Editor: Tony Halliday

Berlitz POCKET GUIDE

Krakow

First Edition 2007
Reprinted 2008

PHOTOGRAPHY
All photography by Gregory Wrona except Sco 59, 60, 64, 66, 73, 74; ATO Picture Archive 13; Bettmann/Corbis 20; Topfoto 57; Stuart Black/The Travel Library 63; Les Gibbon/Alamy 71; Steven May/Alamy 98; Neil Shlecht/Berlitz 99
Cover photograph: Gregory Wrona

CONTACTING THE EDITORS
Every effort has been made to provide accurate information in this publication, but changes are inevitable. The publisher cannot be responsible for any resulting loss, inconvenience or injury. We would appreciate it if readers would call our attention to any errors or outdated information by contacting Berlitz Publishing, PO Box 7910, London SE1 1WE, England.
Fax: (44) 20 7403 0290
Email: berlitz@apaguide.co.uk
<www.berlitzpublishing.com>

Additional research was provided by Kataryzyna Paul and Zuzanna Ananiew

Printed in Singapore by Insight Print Services (Pte) Ltd, 38 Joo Koon Road, Singapore 628990.
Tel: (65) 6865-1600. Fax: (65) 6861-6438

The Planty (page 33) is a restful ring of parkland surrounding the busy streets of the Old Town

The best in Polish fine art, decorative arts, and arms and armour can be seen at the National Museum (page 67)

Medieval St Mary's Basilica (page 26) is impressive inside and out

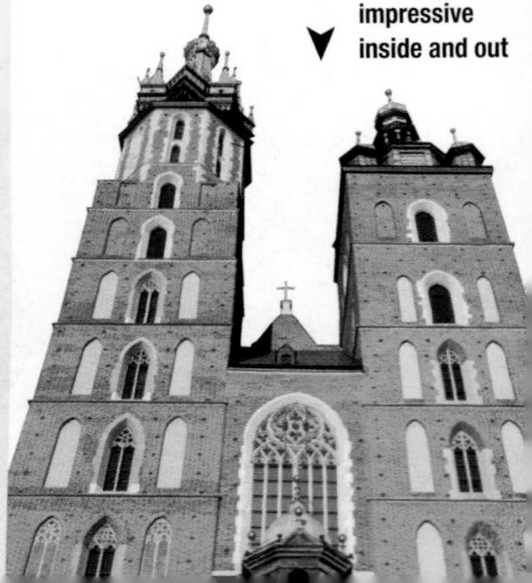

TOP TEN ATTRACTIONS

The focal point of Kazimierz (page 48) is the district's heritage of Jewish life and culture

Kraków's lively heart is the Rynek Główny (page 25), the medieval market square

In the Communist showcase of Nowa Huta, Arka Pana Church (page 62) stands apart as a monument to the Poles' fervent Catholic faith

With its castle and cathedral, kings made Wawel (page 42) the centre of power in Poland for centuries

Near Kraków, Tarnów (page 72) is a perfectly preserved gem of a town

Extraordinary stained-glass designs by Stanisław Wyspiański (page 18)

Confront the face of evil at the Auschwitz death camps (page 70)

CONTENTS

Fact Sheets

Kapelusze

INTRODUCTION

Kraków is considerably more than just cabbages and kings. Poland's magnificent cultural capital and ancient seat of royalty has been mesmerising visitors since the founding of the bishopric of Kraków on Wawel Hill in AD1000. Located in the deep south of Poland, an hour or so north of the spectacular Tatra Mountains and just 100km (62 miles) from the Slovakian border, Kraków has a perfectly preserved UNESCO-protected Old Town, an extraordinary Jewish heritage, bars and clubs in abundance and arguably the best selection of museums and galleries in the country. With attractions like these, it's not hard to see why the city plays host to more than two million visitors a year.

Old Town Treasures

Poland's second city, with just over three-quarters of a million inhabitants, Kraków is one of the main urban areas in the Małopolska (Little Poland) region. At its centre is the only old town in a major Polish city to have escaped complete destruction during World War II. The Old Town's vast market square (Rynek Główny) – the largest in Europe when it was laid out in the Middle Ages – has a dazzling array of glorious buildings. The Renaissance-style Cloth Hall takes pride

While visiting Kraków is hardly expensive, the Kraków Card is still a good deal. Available for two days (45zł) or three (65zł), it gives free access to over 30 museums as well as unlimited travel on public transport. Buy one from the Cultural Information Centre (ul. św. Jana 2; open Mon–Sat 10am–6pm; <www.krakowcard.com>).

Ul. Floriańska in the Old Town

The Rynek Główny, or market square, at the heart of the city

of place at the centre. The surrounding ensemble of buildings includes the twin-towered St Mary's Basilica, built during the 14th–16th centuries. Its beautiful interior will take your breath away.

Leading away from the market square is a beguiling latticework of narrow streets. There are excellent museums and art galleries here; among them, the Czartoryski Museum, a gallery of fine art with a collection that includes a rare painting by Leonardo da Vinci, *Lady with an Ermine*. With deep Catholic traditions, Kraków is the city whose archbishop went on to become Pope John Paul II. The house in which he lived as a young bishop is now the city's Archdiocesan Museum, located along ul. Kanonicza, the Old Town's only street to have been perfectly preserved as it was hundreds of years ago. Encircling the historic centre is the Planty, a delightful wooded park that marks the former location of the medieval city walls.

The Old Town is by no means the only reason to visit Kraków. Wawel, where the country's kings and queens were once crowned and now lie in state in the crypt of the cathedral, is a captivating primer in Polish history. The complex of buildings also includes medieval defensive walls and towers, the royal castle, treasury and armoury.

The nearby district of Kazimierz throws the horrors of World War II into sharp relief. A Jewish community that had thrived for over 450 years was obliterated during the German occupation of Kraków. Kazimierz is now making a comeback as a focal point of Jewish culture and heritage; it's also the city's number-one spot for hedonistic nightlife. Sights such as Kazimierz's Old Synagogue, the oldest surviving synagogue in Poland, and the moving exhibitions inside the Galicia Jewish Museum, rub shoulders with myriad bars and cafés packed nightly with the city's good-looking young things.

Cultural Capital

Formerly the capital of Poland, and home to the country's oldest university (the Jagiellonian), Kraków also lays claim to be Poland's cultural capital. This largely conservative, academic and religious culture has, paradoxically, also nurtured revolutionary artists, such as the city's undisputed genius and leading member of the late 19th-century Young Poland (Młoda Polska) movement, Stanisław Wyspiański. The artist's sideways take on Polish life paved the way for a new generation of social

The trumpeter in the tower of St Mary's Basilica

commentators, who in their turn founded a number of galleries. Wyspiański's work, especially his wonderful stained-glass designs, can be found throughout the city, as well as in the Old Town museum that bears his name. For contemporary art, including the occasional work of genius, the Palace of Fine Arts in the Old Town provides a fine temporary space for the city's up-and-coming artists. Many smaller independent galleries can be found around both the Old Town and in Kazimierz.

Ways to Unwind

When the smoke and noise and chaos of the city get too much, Kraków provides plenty of good choices to slow down and unwind. Summer in Kraków can be a surprisingly hot and sticky affair at times, and city-dwellers seek relief in one of the 40 or so public parks, or, if they're lucky or rich enough, in the surrounding countryside where many like to keep a small summer cottage. Only the brave or

Kraków's Flower Women

The tradition of selling flowers between the Cloth Hall and St Mary's Basilica on Kraków's main market square is believed to have started back in the first half of the 16th century. It is the sole preserve of women known as Krakowskie Kwiaciarki, or the Kraków Flower Women (*kwiat* means 'flower'). There are currently 10 women selling flowers on the square in a business handed down almost exclusively from mother to daughter. Not to be taken lightly, the Kraków Flower Women are highly esteemed in the city, and have traditionally given flowers to visiting VIPS, including Pope John Paul II, Japanese Emperor Hirohito and Prince Charles. It's also their responsibility to lay flowers at the feet of the statue of the Polish author Adam Mickiewicz and hand out mistletoe to passers-by on Christmas Eve.

Relaxing on the bank of the Wisła beside Wawel

foolish take to the city's waters, the River Wisła being little more than a squiggle of pollution that cuts Kraków in two. Located some 600km (375 miles) from the sea, Kraków has few bathing options, apart from the lakes around the city or the massive indoor Water Park (Park Wodny).

The city's Botanical Gardens, the oldest in Poland, provide an opportunity to absorb nature in peaceful surroundings. As well as their tree-lined paths, immaculate gardens, ponds and hothouses, the Botanical Gardens stage concerts during the summer. And for one night only in May, they open their gates after dark as part of the city's delightfully different Museum Night *(see page 25)*.

Beyond the Town Centre

Within easy reach of Kraków's centre is a place that's very recently appeared on the tourist trail. Built just after World War II as a Communist showcase, the industrial district of

A rural view near Zakopane

Nowa Huta draws increasing numbers of visitors to see its monumental socialist-realist architecture.

A short distance southeast of Kraków are the Wieliczka salt mines. In an amazing feat of human labour and creativity, miners have carved solid salt into beautifully ornamented chapels – hundreds of metres below the ground.

There are also options for visitors with time for an extended excursion or two. To the south is Poland's winter capital, Zakopane. During the winter, the small town overflows with skiers from all over the country. Located at the foot of the Tatra Mountains, Zakopane is also very popular in summer, attracting thousands of visitors who use the town as a base for hiking trips and adventures in the pristine mountains and forests surrounding it.

An hour to the east of Kraków is Tarnów, one of the best-preserved medieval towns in Poland. As well as its fascinating streetscape, Tarnów also has two superb wooden churches, not to mention the country's best Gypsy restaurant.

Finally, no trip to Kraków is complete without seeing the former Nazi death camps at Auschwitz, about 75km (47 miles) west of the city. An awkward, uncomfortable and often deeply disturbing experience, a visit to Auschwitz is guaranteed to make a deep impression.

It's this mixture of the tragic and light-hearted, the old and the new, the conservative and the radical that makes Kraków and the area around it such an extraordinary place to visit. Whatever your reason for visiting, your stay in Kraków will provide unique and unforgettable experiences.

A BRIEF HISTORY

The long and complex story of Kraków holds plenty of drama. Over the centuries, Poland's second city and former capital has been invaded, plundered, occupied and destroyed. Each time, the city proved resilient. In times of peace, Kraków has nurtured some of the finest scientific, religious and creative minds in Europe.

Settlers and Invaders

Evidence suggests that what is now Wawel Hill was inhabited by humans 50,000 years ago.

Legend has it that a Slavic duke named Krak founded a fortified settlement on Wawel Hill, which was well positioned on key trade routes. The earliest recorded reference is dated AD965, when Ibrahim ibn Jakub, a merchant from Cordoba in Spain, wrote that 'Krakwa' was a major town known throughout Europe.

Trade bloomed in medieval times

In those days amber was a principal commodity in Kraków. It had been traded since the Neolithic era and was prized in the ancient world for its supposed medicinal benefits. It was also believed to bring the wearer good luck and both youthful-

> **The next time you swing your boot in the direction of one the annoying pigeons in the Rynek, remember this. For reasons that have been lost to time, legend has it that they are none other than the ghosts of the knights and courtiers of Duke Henry (Henryk) IV Probus, senior prince of Poland from 1288 until his death in 1290.**

ness and longevity. Salt from the nearby Wieliczka salt mine was another valuable asset traded from Kraków.

Following Poland's conversion to Christianity in 966, the diocese of Kraków was founded in 1000, with the first cathedral built on Wawel Hill in the early 11th century. Wawel Hill became the royal residence in 1038, when King Kazimierz Odnowiciel (Casimir the Restorer), the patriarch of the Piast dynasty, moved the Polish capital from Gniezno to Kraków. The Tartar invasion of 1241 dealt a blow to this fledgling capital, but it was rapidly rebuilt. The municipal rights it was granted in 1257 established the layout of the centre (which has remained in place), including the Rynek (main market square), the first buildings of the Cloth Hall (Sukiennice), a covered market and the first city walls.

The Golden Age

Under King Kazimierz Wielki (Casimir the Great, 1333–70), the last Piast monarch, Kraków and the country prospered. It is said that Kazimierz found Poland built of wood and left it built of stone. Important buildings erected during his reign include Wawel Castle, which was rebuilt and extended in Gothic style with walls, towers and links to the town's fortifications. Wawel Castle housed the first educational academy, established by the king in 1364, which later became the basis of the city's university. In 1335 he founded the town of Kazimierz, which became part of Kraków in 1800.

In 1386 Władysław Jagiełło, the Grand Duke of Lithuania, was crowned king of Poland after he married the Polish queen, 11-year-old Jadwiga. Thus began the Jagiellonian dynasty (which lasted until 1572) and Poland's union (Commonwealth) with neighbouring Lithuania. On 15 July 1410, the Polish-Lithuianian army defeated the Teutonic Knights at the Battle of Grunwald. The victory was the military and political high point of the Commonwealth.

Kraków thrived under the Jagiellonians. As Europe's trade routes became ever busier, Kraków – strategically placed at the junction between Western Europe and Byzantium, and between Southern Europe and the Baltic and Scandinavia – grew in stature as a capital city and commercial centre.

Its significance was consolidated after it joined the Hanseatic League in 1430. Originally a commercial union of German towns on the Baltic coast, the league went on to promote maritime trade between countries around the Baltic and North seas. By the mid-15th century more than 150 towns were involved, and Kraków took advantage of lucrative trading opportunities. The resulting prosperity prompted German craftsmen and merchants, including Veit Stoss (Wit Stwosz), the master carver of Nuremberg, to visit or move to the town.

Grunwald Monument

The Barbican protected the city during the Renaissance period

The 16th century saw the development of trades and handicrafts, and the formation of 60 guilds. At the beginning of the 16th century, Kraków's printing presses produced the first books printed in Poland; the country's first postal service was established here a few decades later. Following the marriage of King Zygmunt Stary and the Italian princess Bona Sforza in 1518, there was an influx of renowned Italian architects. The legacy of Bartolomeo Berrecci, Giovanni Maria Padua and Santi Gucci can be seen at the Cloth Hall, Wawel Castle, and at various monuments, tombs and epitaphs.

Indeed, Kraków enjoys a distinct Italian Renaissance character. Its medieval defences were also extended at this time. The north of the town was protected by a Barbican and linked by a double-walled thoroughfare to Floriańska Gate, one of eight city gateways.

An Elected Monarch

The Jagiellonian dynasty came to an end in 1572 with the death of King Sigismund II Augustus. The coronation of King Henryk Walezy in 1574 was a minor landmark: he became the first Polish monarch to be elected – albeit by the nobility only – thus marking the end of the country's hereditary system of government. Meanwhile, in the north, Warsaw was also rapidly developing as the capital of the Mazovian dukedom. More central to the Polish-Lithuanian Commonwealth than Kraków, Warsaw was becoming a leading administrative centre. The Sejm (parliament) was transferred to Warsaw in 1569, and Kraków went into decline. In 1596 King Zygmunt III Waza declared Warsaw the Polish capital and transferred the royal residence to Warsaw's Royal Castle. The royal treasury remained at the Wawel, and coronations and royal funerals continued to be held in Wawel Cathedral. King August II was the last king to be crowned here, in 1734.

In 1655–7 Kraków was badly damaged by an invasion by Sweden, one of the Polish-Lithuanian Commonwealth's most powerful rivals. Known locally as Potop ('The Deluge'), the invasion resulted in the looting of the royal treasury and many works of art.

Sarmatism

Sarmatism was the predominant lifestyle and culture of the Polish *szlachta*, or nobility, from the 16th to the 19th century. It was based on the almost certainly fictitious belief that the Poles are the descendants of the Sarmatians, a group of people who lived north of the Black Sea from the 6th century BC to around the 3rd century AD. Polish Sarmatian culture evolved during the Renaissance from a movement of honourable pacifists into a full-blown warrior culture, which valued horse-riding skills and lavish oriental clothing (not to mention vast handlebar moustaches). Sarmatism faded away from the middle of the 18th century, but a pale shadow of it lives on in modern-day Kraków in the form of the Fowler Brotherhood *(see page 64)*. The country's best collection of Sarmatian portraits can be viewed in Tarnów's District Museum *(see page 73)*.

Poland's Decline

The opposition of various nobles to Poland's last king, Stanisław August Poniatowski, elected in 1764, heightened the country's vulnerability to its predatory neighbours. Prussia, Russia and Austro-Hungary partitioned Poland twice, in 1772 and 1793, and the country ceased to exist. Poles united and fought for independence. Tadeusz Koščiuszko took a celebrated oath in Kraków's Rynek before leading his troops to victory over Russia at the Battle of Racławice in 1794. But a third partition, in 1795, forced the king to abdicate. The Kraków region became part of the Austro-

Stanisław Wyspiański

Born in Kraków on 15 January 1869, the architect, painter, playwright, poet and occasional cabinet-maker Stanisław Wyspiański's impact on the city is eclipsed only by God's late representative on Earth and Kraków's most famous son, Pope John Paul II. At the cutting edge of art during his brief lifetime, Wyspiański successfully blended traditional and modern styles to create a new and often controversial way of looking at both Poland under partition and the world in general. He's best remembered for his extraordinary stained-glass designs, several of which can be seen in Kraków. Wyspiański is also famous for writing what's considered by many to be Poland's most important play, *Wesele* (The Wedding), which was turned into a film by the Polish director Andrzej Wajda in 1973. He was a leading member of Young Poland *(Młoda Polska)* art movement (1890–1918), a patriotic collective of artists, writers and musicians whose members included among others Xawery Dunikowski *(see the Palace of Fine Arts on page 37)* and Stanisław Ignacy Witkiewicz, aka Witkacy *(see the Zakopane Style Museum on page 79)*. Plagued by physical and mental illness, Wyspiański died at the age of 38 on 28 November 1907. His body lies in Kraków's Pauline Church *(see page 54)*.

Hungarian Empire. Kazimierz was incorporated into Kraków in 1800.

In 1809 the city became part of the Duchy of Warsaw, established by Napoleon. But in 1815 Napoleon was defeated at Waterloo and the subsequent Congress of Vienna designated Warsaw as the capital of a Russian-ruled Polish 'kingdom'. Kraków was given the status of a free city and capital of the Kraków Republic, which existed until 1846.

Wyspiański's *Act of Creation* in St Francis' Basilica

The Kraków revolution of that year was suppressed by the Austrians, who incorporated the city into their province of Galicia. Under the relatively liberal rule of the Austrians, Polish culture thrived. Then in 1850 the Great Fire of Kraków destroyed or seriously damaged almost 200 buildings, and once again the city had to rebuild. By the turn of the 20th century, Kraków had resumed its role as the country's intellectual and spiritual centre.

Rebirth and Disaster

In 1918, at the end of World War I, a Polish army mobilised in Kraków. Led by Marshal Józef Piłsudski, it defeated the Prussian, Russian and Austro-Hungarian forces. Poland had finally won independence. Piłsudksi acted as head of state until 1922; his state funeral was held in Kraków in 1935.

A Jewish family being transported from their home in 1941

The Nazis invaded Poland on 1 September 1939. They set up a puppet government in Kraków, and the governor general, Hans Frank, took up residence in Wawel Castle. The Płaszów and Liban forced-labour camps were soon constructed, and a number of Jagiellonian University academics were sent to Sachsenhausen concentration camp. A Jewish ghetto was established in Kraków, from where Jews were sent to Auschwitz. There, more than 1 million prisoners, the great majority of them Jews from across Europe, together with Poles, Russians and Roma, died as a result of slavery, hunger, illness, torture or in the gas chambers. Corpses were burned in crematoria and buried in mass graves.

Before retreating in 1944, the Nazis began destroying evidence of their horrific crimes. They detonated the crematoria and some camp buildings, but didn't have enough time to destroy the gas chambers. The Nazis intended to raze Kraków but were foiled by a sudden advance by the Soviet

Red Army. Kraków was thus one of the very few Polish cities to survive the war virtually intact. The Red Army liberated the city in January 1945.

The Postwar Years

The Nazis left Warsaw devastated, so for a short time Kraków was once again the country's premier city. Rigged elections resulted in a Communist government, and the country became a satellite of the Soviet Union. The new regime was determined to replace the city's intellectual and cultural elitism with a new socialist spirit in the form of a vast proletarian labour force. The Lenin Steelworks, now known as Sendzimir, were built in the Kraków suburb of Nowa Huta in 1947–9.

A key opponent of the repressive regime was the Catholic Church, which retained a level of independence during the Cold War years. The investiture of the archbishop of Kraków, Karol Wojtyła, as Pope John Paul II in 1978, and his visit to Poland in 1979, boosted opposition elements.

Lech Wałesa's Solidarity movement mounted the most serious threat to an Eastern bloc regime since the Prague Spring of 1968. Bowing to the sheer weight of its numbers and international support, the government accepted it as a legal trade union in 1980. But the following year, General Jaruzelski introduced martial law and declared Solidarity abolished. This was a time of severe shortages – people had to queue all night for staples – and meat, butter

It's hard to overstate the importance of the Catholic Church in Poland, a fact made clear in 1978 when Karol Wojtyła, the Polish cardinal and archbishop of Kraków, was elected to the papacy. Pope John Paul II was the first non-Italian to get the top job for over 400 years.

and even vodka were rationed. Artificial employment provided work, however menial or unnecessary, for everyone. Martial law was lifted in 1983, triggered by the second visit to his homeland of John Paul II.

Waves of strikes in the spring and autumn of 1988 led to talks between the Communist Party and the leaders of Solidarity. A path towards democracy was mapped out. The Communists were soundly beaten in the election of June 1989, and the Communist Party was dissolved in January 1990. Privatisation of state-run companies began in 1994.

The newly independent country began to look outwards. Poland joined NATO in 1999 and the European Union in 2004. Kraków served as European City of Culture in 2000.

Today's Kraków

The economic reforms and rise in living standards that Poland has experienced since 1989 have been particularly noticeable in Kraków. Café society has returned, restaurants have boomed, shops stock top international brand names and premium-quality Polish products, and standards of service have improved. Pollution from the Nowa Huta steelworks – detrimental to people and historic buildings alike – has been reduced. The annual Jewish Festival of Culture, begun in 1988 as a small academic gathering, has blossomed into a major event, reviving the city's Jewish heritage. Above all, Kraków is now firmly on the international tourist map – over 2 million people visit each year.

A youngster in traditional dress

Historical Landmarks

50,000BC People are living in the Wawel Hill area.
9000–4500BC Tribes of hunter-gatherers appear in the Kraków area.
AD965 Cordoba merchant Ibrahim ibn Jakub refers to a city called Krakwa.
990 Kraków is incorporated into Poland by Bolesław I the Brave who builds Wawel and the city's first cathedral.
1000 The diocese of Kraków is founded.
1038 Casimir the Restorer moves his capital to Kraków from Gniezno.
1257 Kraków is granted municipal rights by Bolesław the Shy.
1333 Casimir the Great, the last of the Piast dynasty, is crowned king.
1335 Casimir the Great founds Kazimierz.
1397 St Mary's Basilica is completed.
1364 Kraków Academy (today's Jagiellonian University) is founded.
1386 Lithuanian Grand Duke Władysław Jagiełło is crowned king.
1430 Kraków joins the Hanseatic League.
1494 Kraków's Jews are forced to move into neighbouring Kazimierz.
1574 Henryk Walezy becomes Poland's first elected king.
1596 The nation's capital is moved from Kraków to Warsaw.
1772 First partition of Poland.
1793 Second partition of Poland.
1794 Koščiuszko Uprising begins.
1795 Third partition of Poland, which ceases to exist. Kraków becomes part of the Austro-Hungarian Empire.
1918 Poland regains independence; Kraków is the first major free city in the new republic.
1939–44 The Nazis murder most of Kraków's large Jewish population.
1945 Imposition of Communist rule.
1978 Karol Wojtyła becomes Pope John Paul II. Kraków is put on the UNESCO World Heritage list.
1981 Imposition of martial law by General Jaruzelski.
1989 Talks between the government and Solidarity lead to elections.
2000 Kraków becomes the European City of Culture.
2004 Poland joins the European Union.

WHERE TO GO

Most visitors to Kraków are drawn to its Old Town, one of the most beautiful in Europe and the only major old town in Poland to escape destruction in World War II. The two other major sights, Wawel and Kazimierz, are immediately south of the Old Town, making exploration of Kraków very easy. Off the major tourist trail lie a number of treasures, ranging from some of the city's best museums to the emerging Holocaust trail in Podgórze, south of the Wisła. The eastern district of Nowa Huta provides a snapshot of Poland's Communist past, while to the west, in the town of Oświęcim, are the former Nazi death camps at Auschwitz. Southeast of the city in Wieliczka are the extraordinary, UNESCO-protected salt mines. Further afield, towns such as Tarnów and the mountain resort of Zakopane offer those with time on their hands a chance to experience the region to the full.

For one night every May, many of Kraków's museums open until midnight or later, presenting their usual exhibits in an unusual way. Highlights include the amazing Night of the Hassidim in Kazimierz's Old Synagogue, and a wonderful chance to see the Botanical Gardens in a new light. Tickets can be bought from the Cultural Information Centre ***(see page 81).***

THE OLD TOWN: RYNEK GŁÓWNY

Among Poland's impressive market squares, Kraków's immense 200m x 200m (656ft x 656ft) Rynek Główny is the undisputed king. The focal point of Kraków's wonderful Old Town (Stare Miasto), and an ideal starting point for exploring the city, the Rynek was laid out in 1257, and at the time was the largest square in Europe. Long a thriving centre of commerce, the Rynek retains this commercial bustle, while also being the city's primary tourist magnet. It offers a host of things to see and do as well as providing a ring of outdoor cafés for sitting and watching the world go by during the summer months.

St Mary's Basilica

Of the two main sights fighting for supremacy (the other being the magnificent Cloth Hall), the twin-towered **St Mary's Basilica** (Kościół Mariacki; open daily 11.30am–6pm; admission fee) in the square's northeastern corner has a slight edge over its commercial cousin. The Gothic exterior dates from the 14th century, although what really makes this church one of the city's major highlights is found inside. The colour and intricacy of the triple-naved interior is breathtaking; it includes 19th-century murals by Jan Matejko, extraordinary stained glass by Stanisław Wyspiański and a massive late-Gothic altarpiece called *The Lives of Our Lady and Her Son Jesus Christ*, which was completed between 1477–89 by the German master carver Veit Stoss (Wit Stwosz).

The view from the northernmost **tower** (open May–Aug Tues, Thur and Sat 9–11.30am and 1–5.30pm; admission fee) is worth the struggle up the 239 steps. Every day, on the hour, a trumpeter sounds his horn from here. The abrupt pause recalls a legendary watchman who, on sighting Tartar invaders, raised the alarm and was silenced by an arrow.

St Mary's Basilica

The ornate interior of St Mary's Basilica

Next to St Mary's on Plac Mariacki is **St Barbara's Church** (Kościół św. Barbary). Dating from the 14th or 15th century, this was the main Polish site of worship in the city under Austrian occupation, when German was still the main language in use in the basilica next door. Just outside the entrance on the left is a 16th-century sculpture of *Gethsemane*, while inside the main points of interest are the 15th-century stone *Pietà* and the superb 18th-century painted ceiling.

Cloth Hall

At the centre of the Rynek is the imposing **Cloth Hall** (Sukiennice; open Mon–Fri 10am–7pm, Sat and Sun 10am–6pm), which started life as a small shed for storing goods around the time the Rynek was laid out. The Cloth Hall's current appearance owes most to the Italian architect Giovanni il Mosca, who in the 16th century gave it its predominantly Renaissance look. Today's Cloth Hall is home to a ground-floor **market** selling

Hunting for jewellery among open-air market stalls

folk crafts, jewellery, leather goods and souvenirs, and the superb **Noworolski Café** *(see page 101)*. Upstairs is the usual location of a **gallery** of 19th-century Polish paintings, which includes the work of one of Poland's greatest painters, Jan Matejko. The collection is temporarily housed in the Royal Castle in Niepołomice, 25km (15 miles) east of Kraków.

Town Hall Tower

On the other side of the building is a branch of the Kraków Historical Museum, housed inside the **Town Hall Tower** (Wieża Ratuszowa; open May–Oct daily 10.30am–2pm and 2.30–6pm; admission fee). The tower is all that remains of the 14th-century Town Hall, ravaged by fire and pulled down by the Austrians in the early 19th century. The 68m (223ft) tower is now home to a **Tourist Information Centre** and a small collection of old photographs and clothing. A 110-step climb takes you to a **viewing platform** offering an excellent panorama.

Beside the tower is an odd-looking sculpture of a head on its side that on closer inspection can be entered and explored. This is ***Eros Bendato***, the work of the German-born Polish sculptor Igor Mitorraj (1944–), who studied at Kraków's Academy of Art. Originally a painter, Mitoraj's sculptures are all based on the human form and most feature bandages of some description, looking at the same time like fractured contemporary visions and broken statues of antiquity. Two smaller pieces can be seen in the National Museum *(see page 67)*.

Other Sights in the Rynek

The diminutive **St Adalbert's Church** (Kościół św. Wojciecha) is to the southeast of the Cloth Hall. The earliest parts of the building date back to the 11th century, making it older than the Rynek and every other church in the city. It's a beguiling jumble of pre-Roman, Roman, Gothic, Renaissance and Baroque. Inside, just six rows of humble wooden pews are arranged on a floor that sits some 2m (6½ft) below the surface of the surrounding market square. A glass floor has been built around two edges of the church to give an impression of how the building once looked.

Immediately east of the Cloth Hall is the **Adam Mickiewicz Monument** (Pomnik Adama Mickiewicza), one of the most famous statues in Poland. Strangely enough, the country's foremost 19th-century Romantic poet never visited Kraków and is claimed by the Lithuanians (who call him

St Adalbert's, the Adam Mickiewicz Monument and the Cloth Hall

The Rynek brims with outdoor cafés in the summer months

Adomas Mickevičius) as one of their own. Mickiewicz's most famous work, the epic poem *Pan Tadeusz*, opens with the line 'Lithuania, my country!', adding to the confusion. The poet died in Paris in 1855. Thirty-five years later his remains were bought to Kraków and laid to rest in the crypt of Wawel Cathedral, an event that inspired a competition to build the monument, which was won by Teodor Rygier. Rygier's work, unveiled in 1898 to celebrate the centenary of the poet's birth, was destroyed by the Germans during World War II. The current statue dates from 1955 and is a popular meeting place.

Around the Edges

The Rynek's scores of cafés are located in superb merchant houses, all of which have a story to tell. Of particular interest is the building at **no. 9**, the one-time home of Kraków's multitalented artist Stanisław Wyspiański *(see page 18)*, and, in the far northwestern corner, the main branch of the **Kraków Historical Museum** (open Wed–Sun 10am–5.30pm; admission fee). Founded in 1899, the museum is housed inside Italian architect Baldassare Fontana's spectacular Pałac Pod Krzysztofory (Palace Under St Christopher). The upstairs features a permanent exhibition tracing the history of the city from the year it received its royal charter in 1257 until the German invasion of 1939. Among the many exhibits are some fine pieces of furniture and a collection of oil portraits of some of the city's more famous historical characters inside the opulent Fontana Room. There's also a stirring exhibit that tells the story of Poland's struggle for independence at the end of World War I.

Just off the Rynek, opposite St Mary's Basilica, is the highly recommended **Burgher Museum** (open Wed, Fri–Sun 9am–4pm, Thur noon–7pm; admission fee). Also known as the **Hippolit House** (Kamienica Hipolitów) after a rich 16th-century merchant family who once lived in the building. Each room has been painstakingly set out with authentic furniture from the 17th century until the first half of the 20th century. The entrance is found inside the hallway next to the tourist information centre. Colourful façades adorn nearby **Little Market Square** (Mały Rynek), once the site of meat, fish and poultry vendors.

Lenin in Kraków

On a bright midsummer morning on 22 June 1912, Vladimir Ilyich Lenin arrived in Kraków on the overnight train from Vienna. He wished to be closer to his beloved Russia, whose borders, at the time, ran just a few kilometres to the north. Living in a rented apartment with his wife and mother-in-law, the 42-year-old divided his time between planning a revolution, eating smoked salmon, listening to Beethoven, visiting Noworolski Café *(see page 101)* and, during the harsh Polish winters, ice-skating near the city's Botanical Gardens.

Lenin spent his two Galician summers in the village of Poronin near Zakopane, where he organised a conference of Bolshevik leaders. Agents infiltrated the conference and arranged for his arrest by the Austrian police as a Russian spy on 8 August 1914. Briefly imprisoned, Lenin was soon released and left for Switzerland, never to return. His two years in the city are described in *Lenin in Kraków* by Jan Adamczewski which, though only available in Polish, is well worth tracking down, even if it requires marrying a Pole who can read it to you.

Street scene in the Old Town

THE OLD TOWN: AROUND THE RYNEK

What is now known as the Old Town was founded by Bolesław the Shy (1226–79) and built to replace a group of small settlements destroyed by the Tartar invasion of 1241. The Old Town received its municipal (Magdeberg Law) rights in 1257. It was populated by settlers primarily from the German-speaking region of Silesia, and was for its first few years a city ruled by Germans. Kraków's Polishness began on 1 September 1306, when an army led by Władysław the Short (1261–1333) invaded the city, leaving 2,000 dead Germans in its wake. Fifteen years later, on 20 January 1319, Władysław the Short was crowned king of Poland in Wawel Cathedral, and thus began Kraków's so-called Golden Age.

Somewhat surprisingly, much of the city's wonderful grid-like Old Town remains relatively untouched by the creeping claws of tourism. Around the Rynek is a marvellous higgledy-piggledy collection of fine old buildings in all states of repair, from crumbling ruins to newly renovated structures. These buildings house everything from some of Poland's best museums to the occasional saucy nightclub. The Old Town's best sights and institutions are described below. A highly recommended way to supplement your visit is to go for a lazy wander through the quiet back-streets, which are lined with historic town houses, fine churches and delightful small shops.

The Old Town's **Royal Route** (Trakt Królewski) is the traditional route that new Polish kings and queens took to their coronations. Splitting the Old Town more or less neatly in two from north to south, it starts at the Barbican *(see page 34)*, runs down ul. Floriańska, through the Rynek and south along ul. Grodzka to Wawel *(see page 42)*.

Encircling the whole of the Old Town is the **Planty**, a ring of relaxing parklands *(see box opposite)*. The Planty marks the former location of massive fortifications and a wide moat that once protected the city from attack.

Of the 40 or so parks in Kraków, the Planty, a wonderful 21-hectare (52-acre) ring of green around the Old Town, is the most obvious choice for an escape from the incessant racket of the city centre. Situated on the site of the city's former medieval defensive walls, knocked down in the early part of the 19th century, it is made up of some 30 individual gardens and is full of trees, sculptures and, in summer, several cafés.

A section of the Barbican

Around the Barbican and Ul. Floriańska

At the far northern end of ul. Floriańska, through the 14th-century Brama Floriańska (Florian's Gate), is the **Barbican** (Barbakan; open May–Oct daily 10.30am–6pm; admission fee). Built in 1498, this fort was once the city's northern defence point. With its seven turrets and walls 3m (10ft) thick, the Barbican is, along with Florián's Gate, the oldest surviving part of the city's medieval defences. Visitors can walk around the two ramparts, and there's a small exhibition in the main courtyard.

Just northeast of the Barbican, and not technically part of the Old Town, is the large **Grunwald Monument** (Pomnik Grunwaldzki) on pl. Matejki. The Battle of Grunwald (in German 'Tannenberg', in Lithuanian 'Žalgiris') took place between a combined Polish-Lithuanian army and the Teutonic Knights on 15 July 1410 and resulted in the defeat of the Knights. One of Poland's proudest moments, the battle was commemorated on its 500th anniversary in 1910 by the unveiling of this monument in front of an estimated 160,000 people. It features the Polish king Władysław Jagiełło riding his horse and flanked by representatives of the Polish and Lithuanian armies. At the front, directly underneath Jagiełło, is his cousin, the Lithuanian prince Vytautas (Witold), and beneath him lies a deceased Urlich von Jungingen, the Teutonic Knights' Grand Master. The current statue is a copy from 1976, made from models and drawings of the original destroyed by the occupying Germans during World War II.

Back on ul. Floriańska and south past the Barbican on the left-hand side is the **Jan Matejko House** (Dom Jana Matejki; open Wed, Thur and Sun 10am–3.30pm, Fri 10am–6pm; admission fee). The artist Jan Matejko was born here in 1838. A one-time teacher of Stanisław Wyspiański *(see page 18)*, Matejko won a place in the heart of the nation with his vast oil paintings depicting epic moments from Polish history. Pictures, documents and personal possessions celebrate the artist's life.

Further down ul. Floriańska is the quirky **Pharmacy Museum** (Muzeum Farmacji; open Tues 3pm–7pm, Wed–Sun 11am–2pm; admission fee), a beautifully restored, 15th-century burgher house stuffed full of recreations of old apothecaries, jars of pickled snakes and other medicine-related odds and ends. Of particular interest is the small exhibit dedicated to the pharmacist Tadeusz Pankiewicz *(see box on page 56)*, the only Gentile permitted to live in the Kraków ghetto during World War II.

Mortar and pestle stained glass at the Pharmacy Museum

In the northeastern corner of the Old Town on pl. św. Ducha is the wedding-cake **Juliusz Słowacki Theatre** (Teatr im. Juliusza Słowackiego). Styled on the Paris Opera and controversially built on the site of a medieval church demolished to make way for it, it was opened in 1893 and hides a few lavish treats inside. It's not officially open for tours, but if you attend a theatre or opera performance here *(see page 81)*, you'll see the gilded interior.

Czartoryski Museum

Just to the west of the Floriańska Gate on ul. św. Jana, some of the city's finest works of art can be found inside the ➤ **Czartoryski Museum** (Muzeum Czartoryskich; open Wed, Fri and Sat 10am–6pm, Tues, Thur and Sun 10am–3.30pm; admission fee). Works include some beautiful religious paintings from the 14th century, a fine military collection,

Czartoryski Museum, notable for its Leonardo da Vinci piece

and Leonardo da Vinci's *Lady with an Ermine*, one of only a handful of the artist's paintings on public display in the world. Beyond the artworks on show is simply the interest of visiting a palace belonging to one of Kraków's most prominent families, who were collectors on a grand scale.

The best locally published book about the Old Town is the pocket-sized *Kraków's Old Town* (Wydawnictwo Bezdroża, 2004). This little pink masterpiece covers the history of the Old Town and describes six individual walking tours. Passionate and humorous, the book is just 35zł. Copies can be bought from Empik *(see page 119)* and other bookshops around town.

On the corner of ul. św. Jana and ul. św. Tomasza is the diminutive **Church of St John the Baptist and St John the Evangelist** (Kościół św. Jana Chrzciciela i św. Jana Ewangelisty). The church predates the Old Town, which accounts for the kink in the road immediately south of the building (known to the locals as the Doubting Thomas Nook). However, the original 12th-century Romanesque building was extensively remodelled (to the point of being almost entirely rebuilt) during the first half of the 17th century, which explains the church's Baroque appearance. The interior is relatively plain, the main interest being the 16th-century altar painting, *The Mother of God Redeeming the Slaves*.

The Palace of Fine Art and Wyspiański Museum

Situated on pl. Szczepański in the northwest is the **Palace of Fine Art** (Pałac Sztuki; open Mon–Fri 8.15am–6pm, Sat–Sun 10am–6pm; admission fee). The early 20th-century neo-Baroque building hosts hit-and-miss exhibitions of contemporary art, and is the city's most active nurturer of new artists. It also contains a lovely wooden bust of Xawery

Dunikowski (1875–1964) holding a tiny church in his hand in the entrance hall. Dunikowski was an artist and sculptor who lived a long and fascinating life. An Auschwitz survivor, his death camp-inspired art and other work in general is worth looking out for.

➤ Opposite, the **Wyspiański Museum** (Muzeum Stanisław a Wyspiańskiego; open Tues, Thur and Fri 10am–3.30pm, Wed and Sat 10am–6pm; admission fee) celebrates the life and art of Stanisław Wyspiański *(see page 18)*. Exhibits include personal possessions, original drawings, some wonderful stained-glass designs and Wyspiański's vision of Wawel Hill in the form of an extraordinary model *(see page 44)*. The museum is best visited with the aid of the pamphlet or booklet, which can be bought from the ticket office. The museum also has a nice café in the courtyard in summer.

Jagiellonian University

A short walk west of the Rynek is the **Jagiellonian University Museum** (Muzeum Uniwersytetu Jagiellońskiego; open Mon, Wed and Fri 10am–2.20pm, Tues and Thur 10am–5.20pm, Sat 10am–2pm; admission fee; advance booking recommended, tel: 012 422 05 49). It's housed in the **Collegium Maius**, Europe's third-oldest (and Poland's first) university college, having been founded in 1364. Nicolas Copernicus (Mikolaj Kopernik), who formulated our modern theory of the solar system, is believed to have begun studying here in 1492.

The museum, which contains a wealth of artefacts from the university's collection, can only be seen on a guided tour. Starting from a gorgeous courtyard, tours take in the best of the interiors – including ornate academic halls, the treasury, library and professors' dining hall – as well as objects such as oil paintings, ancient books and a range of old scientific instruments. One of the most precious possessions is the oldest globe depicting the Americas still in existence.

On tour in the courtyard of the Collegium Maius

Basilica of St Francis and Dominican Church

On either side of ul. Grodzka, at the intesection with pl. Wszystkich Świętych, are two particularly impressive churches. To the west, the **Basilica of St Francis of Assisi** (Bazylika św. Franciszka z Asyżu) was the first brick building in the city when it was constructed in 1269. Like so many other houses of worship in the city, the basilica has seen numerous structural and decorative changes over the centuries, including the addition of several Wyspiański stained-glass windows installed between 1895 and 1904 at the front and back of the building. This is perhaps the best place to see his work in all its glory. The large *Act of Creation* depicts God in wild streaks of colour *(see picture on page 19)*; Wyspiański is believed to have based the face of God on that of a beggar. The walls and ceiling are covered in bright Art Nouveau designs, which are radical almost beyond belief, especially set against the austere Gothic wooden confessionals.

Outside the Basilica of St Francis

Head east from here to the imposing **Dominican Church** (Kościół Dominikanów), which is located on the site of the city's original marketplace. The church was completed in around 1250 and originally belonged to an order of monks from Bologna. The lavish interior was gutted by fire in 1850 and remodelled in a far more sober manner in 1872. Of particular interest inside the immense building are the huge Gothic wooden altars and the image of *Our Lady of the Rosary* inside the Rosary Chapel, which is reputed to have special healing powers.

South along Ul. Grodzka

You'll find a couple of diversions in the area immediately southwest of pl. Wszystkich Świętych and ul. Grodzka, courtesy of two of Kraków's less well-known museums. Of narrow appeal is the very small **Geology Museum** (Muzeum Geologiczne; open Thur–Fri 10am–3pm, Sat 10am–2pm; admission fee) on ul. Senacka. It consists of a handful of glass cases full of various rocks and crystals found in the Kraków area. The exhibits are labelled in Polish only.

Around the corner, on ul. Poselska, is the larger and far better **Archaeology Museum** (Muzeum Archeologiczne; open Mon–Wed and Sat 9am–2pm, Thur 2pm–6pm, Fri 10am–2pm; admission fee). Exhibits include models showing how life looked in the Małopolska region of southern Poland over the past several thousand years, an outstanding collection of local clothing from 70,000BC up until the construction of the Old Town, and a few rooms given over to ancient Egypt. The museum looks much better for a recent cash injection.

Ss Peter and Paul's Church

On the eastern side of ul. Grodzka is **Ss Peter and Paul's Church** (Kościół św. Piotra i św. Pawła), an early 16th-century Baroque masterpiece. Kraków's main Jesuit church has changed hands numerous times over the centuries, but is now back with its rightful owners. The striking statues of the Twelve Apostles guarding the entrance are copies of the 18th-century originals. The crypt contains the remains of the priest, Piotr Skarga (1536–1612), whose controversial statue, looking not unlike a posing Elvis Presley, stands in the small square just across the street.

The Twelve Apostles atop Ss Peter and Paul's Church

Ul. Kanonicza

Originally part of a tiny hamlet called Okół that became a part of Kraków in 1410, **ul. Kanonicza**, which runs parallel to ul. Grodzka, is the one street in the Old Town that's been kept as it was, with no annoying signs, glitzy shops or burger bars. The street is sacred to the Poles as being the former home of a young and rather sporty Karol Wojtyła, who became Pope John Paul II in 1978 after serving as archbishop of Kraków.

Much of the street belongs to the Catholic Church, including Wojtyła's former seminary, now the city's **Archdiocesan Museum** (Muzeum Archidiecezjalne; open Tues–Fri 10am–4pm, Sat and Sun 10am–3pm; admission fee) at no. 19. It's brimming with religious goodies from the 13th century to the present day.

WAWEL

Wawel is Poland's grand symbol of patriotism, independence, pride and hope, an extraordinary ensemble of buildings perched on top of a 50m (165ft) rock at the southern tip of the Old Town. The complex offers an A–Z of Polish history and nobility within the pleasurable confines of its four fortified walls, containing a wealth of exhibits inside its mostly Romanesque and Gothic structures.

Tucked away between the information centre and Lost Wawel *(see page 47)* on the ensemble's southeast wall is Musica Antiqua (open daily 10am–6pm), a tiny shop selling classical records and CDs. There are currently no recordings of music performed in the cathedral, but some are promised.

Evidence exists of human life on Wawel Hill 50,000 years ago. The first major structure on the site was the first cathedral, built in 1020. Major construction work on the buildings as they're more or less known today began when Kraków became the

'Here everything is Poland, every stone and fragment' (Wyspiański)

Polish capital in 1038, and numerous additions were made in subsequent centuries. Wawel's most notable features date from the period 1507–36, when the Italians Francesco the Florentine and Bartolomeo Berrecci oversaw a major series of changes. In World War II, the Nazis made Wawel their headquarters, and the area narrowly escaped being turned to rubble when they retreated.

Wawel's popularity means that visiting, especially during the busy summer tourist season, has been limited to a certain number of tourists each day, making booking in advance highly recommended (tel: 012 422 16 97). Wawel covers a large area, so be sure to pick up a free map at the information centre *(see page 47)* when you visit. The full Wawel experience can take at least a day if everything is taken in and enjoyed at a leisurely pace. If time is limited, be sure to visit at least the cathedral and, inside the castle, the Crown Treasury and Armoury.

The Cathedral

➤ An unmissable sight is the **cathedral** (katedra; open Mon–Sat 9am–5pm, Sun 12.15pm–5pm; admission fee only for the crypt and bell tower). A cathedral was built here in 1020, soon after the founding of the diocese of Kraków. The current cathedral, technically the third to stand on the site, dates primarily from the 14th century and is considered by many to be the most important building in the country. Although less impressive than St Mary's Basilica, Wawel Cathedral is by no means an underachiever, and features a wealth of statues, chapels and tombs among its highlights. Dominating everything as you enter is the grand tomb of the former bishop of Kraków, St Stanisław (1030–79), who, according to legend, was murdered by Bolesław II the Bold, and to whom the cathedral is dedicated.

The Wawel-Akropolis

Stanisław Wyspiański's connections with Kraków include an extensive attachment to Wawel dating back to childhood. Wawel features in many of his works, including poems, his first play, *Legend* (1898), and a number of unfulfilled designs for Wawel Cathedral. His masterpiece was a complete redesign of the castle complex, the 'Wawel-Akropolis', motivated by the Austrian army's plans to move their barracks out of Wawel and into new premises. Throughout the winter of 1904–5 Wyspiański, with the help of the architect Władysław Ekielski, worked on a project to remove the parts of Wawel built by the Austrian occupiers, and add a series of buildings, towers and even an amphitheatre. His intention was to create a vision of Poland as the mighty nation it once was. Illness prevented progress beyond a series of drawings, and the work was never completed. A spectacular model based on Wyspiański's sketches was made in the early 1980s and is now a major exhibit at the Wyspiański Museum *(see page 38)*.

The cathedral contains a total of 18 chapels. Each one has its own intrinsic beauty, but the most spectacular is the 15th-century Holy Cross Chapel (on the right as you enter), complete with some extraordinary Russian murals painted in 1470. Also in this chapel is Kazimierz IV's 1492 marble sarcophagus, the work of Veit Stoss.

St Zygmunt Bell

Entrance to the main building is free. You have to pay for a full visit, which takes in the **Royal Crypts** and a trip up the winding wooden stairs to view the 11-tonne **St Zygmunt Bell**. The crypts are where 10 of Poland's former kings and their wives, as well as many other important figures, including the poet and patriot Adam Mickiewicz and Poland's military hero Józef Piłsudki, lie in their tombs. The massive bell was cast in 1520, and can be heard some 50km (31 miles) away. You can buy your tickets from the ticket office opposite the cathedral's main (western) entrance.

The adjoining **Cathedral Museum** (Muzeum Katedralne; open Tues–Sun 10am–3pm; admission fee) was opened in 1978 by Karol Wojtyła immediately prior to his accession to the papacy. A highly recommended diversion, it contains some of Poland's most precious religious and regal possessions, dating from the 13th century onwards. The Cathedral Museum is best enjoyed with a visit to the Archdiocesan Museum *(see page 42)* if you want to get the full flavour and significance of the long relationship between the city and the Church.

Smok Wawelski, the fire-breathing dragon of legend

Castle Highlights

At the eastern edge of the Renaissance-style courtyard are the **State Rooms** (Reprezentacyjne Komnaty Królewskie) and **Royal Private Apartments** (Prywatne Apartamenty Królewskie; open Tues–Sat 9.30am–4pm; admission fee; access by guided tour only). On display in a seemingly never-ending series of breathtaking rooms are intricate carved furniture, some wonderful oil portraits and a series of huge and delightful 16th-century Flemish tapestries. Highlights of the State Rooms include the magnificent Bird Room, the Eagle Hall and the Senators' Hall. Keep an eye out for the extraordinary medieval wallpaper.

Located in the northeastern corner of the courtyard, to the left of the State Rooms, is another highly recommended sight, the **Crown Treasury and Armoury** (Skarbiec Koronny i Zbrojownia; open Tues–Sat 9.30am–4pm, Sun 10am–4pm; admission fee). The most renowned exhibit is *Szczerbiec* ('notched sword'), Poland's original (12th- or 13th-century) coronation sword, but each room here contains a great many other pieces of interest. Among the treasures are Poland's Crown Jewels, intricately etched golden platters and goblets, old coins and a frightening, albeit dazzling, array of military equipment. There's a room full of huge spears, a collection of delightfully detailed and ornate saddles, several walls lined with crossbows, and a cellar containing cannons galore and reproductions of the banners captured at the Battle of Grunwald *(see page 15)*.

To the west on the other side of the courtyard wall is **Lost Wawel** (Zaginiony Wawel; open Mon, Wed and Thur 9.30am–4pm, Tues and Fri 9am–5pm, Sat 11am–6pm, Sun 10am–4pm; admission fee). This museum features archaeological finds from Wawel, as well as newer pieces, laid out in five rooms. The well-presented exhibits include medieval coins, remains of the castle's former royal kitchens and a Renaissance altar from Wawel Cathedral. The museum also has an exceptional multimedia show depicting how Wawel is believed to have looked between the 10th and 12th centuries.

More information about Wawel can be found online at <www.wawel.krakow.pl>, or you can visit the **information centre** in the southwest corner of the complex (open Mon–Fri 9am–6pm, Sat and Sun 9am–6pm), which also has a gift shop, small post office and café.

'Ere Be Dragons

Like all old cities, Kraków has a number of legends. One of them concerns a mythical dragon by the name of Smok Wawelski, who lived in a cave on Wawel and favoured a life of dining on sheep and alarming the occasional virgin. The hero of the story is none other than Krak, the founder of the city. Handsome and clever, Krak fooled the dragon (nobody knows exactly how) into eating a tar-stuffed sheep, which subsequently exploded, to the delight of the local farm animals and young ladies. A six-legged metal statue of Smok Wawelski that periodically breathes gas flames stands outside the dragon's supposed former cave (open daily May–Nov 10am–6pm; admission fee).

By the River Wisła

Between Wawel and the Wisła is a small strip of parkland by the river known as **Bulwar Czerwieński**, which is popular in the summer with the locals as a place to lie in the sun and do nothing. If you're feeling active, you can follow the river on foot or by bike to Kazimierz. In the high season, boats moored by the river bank sell food and drink.

Directly across the water is the quirky **Manggha** (ul. Konopnickiej 26; open Tues–Sun 10am–6pm; admission fee). Part of the National Museum, Manggha is made up primarily of the personal collection of Japanese art of Feliks Jasienski (1861–1929). The museum also has a café selling green tea, a small shop and a pleasant terrace next to the river.

KAZIMIERZ

Kazimierz was founded in the 14th century as a town in its own right, a commercial rival to the German-dominated Kraków less than 1km (⅔ mile) to the north. Over the centuries, it has seen the best and worst of life. It's best-known as the one-time home of Kraków's thriving religious and secular Jewish communities, a fame that stems in part from the huge global success of the movie *Schindler's List*, much of which was filmed in and around Kazimierz. The delightfully scruffy district's contemporary reputation as a centre for all things cutting-edge, arty and bohemian has breathed new life into what was until recently a fairly uneventful place to visit.

The star of David in Kazimierz's Tempel Synagogue

Café and restaurant on ul. Szeroka

Kazimierz's unique mix of Jewish heritage and offbeat bars offers a refreshing alternative to the Old Town.

Jewish Kazimierz

At the time of the German invasion of 1939, Kraków had been home to a rich Jewish tradition for some 700 years. Almost all of the city's 60,000 Jews (25 percent of the city's population) lived in Kazimierz. On 3 March 1941, the Germans began moving the Jewish population into the ghetto in Podgórze, just south of Kazimierz *(see page 55)*. By the time Kraków was liberated by the Red Army in January 1945, an entire Orthodox, Hassidic and secular culture had been destroyed; only about 2,000 Kraków Jews were still alive. Today, a revival of Jewish culture is under way in Kazimierz, and there's plenty to see. Information about the annual international Jewish festival can be found on *page 91*.

The ornate interior of Tempel Synagogue *(see page 52)*

Around Ul. Szeroka

The nucleus of Kazimierz's Jewish revival can be found along **ul. Szeroka**, which is more of a square than a street. Here you'll find the main Jewish restaurants, as well as some good places to pick up books and information. At the southern end is the **Old Synagogue** (Stara Synagoga; open Mon, Wed, Thur 10am–4pm, Fri 10am–5pm; admission fee). The earliest parts of Poland's oldest surviving synagogue date from the start of the 15th century, but many alterations have taken place over the centuries. The red-brick neo-Renaissance building is rather plain on the outside; the real focus of interest is the interior, which is now a museum of Jewish heritage and culture. Photos, relics and Adam Muszka's (1914–2005) superb painting, *Seder Supper*, are among the exhibits. A small bookshop can be found in what was once the women's section of the synagogue.

North along ul. Szeroka is the **Remuh Synagogue** (open Sun–Fri 9am–6pm; admission fee). Kraków's last working

Orthodox synagogue was built in 1553 and has been completely renovated. This magnificent little building is also the site of the city's oldest remaining Jewish cemetery, which was used to bury the city's illustrious Jewish citizens until it was replaced by the New Jewish Cemetery in 1800 *(see page 52)*. Among those laid to rest here is the renowned 16th-century writer and philosopher Rabbi Moses Isserles, known as Remuh, whose son founded the synagogue.

To the east on ul. Dajwór at No. 18 is the highly recommended **Galicia Jewish Museum** (Galicja Muzeum; open daily 9am–7pm; admission fee). The museum, which occupies a former Jewish-owned factory, opened in 2004 and features an excellent permanent exhibition of contemporary photographs of the remnants of Jewish culture in Galicia (the old name for southern Poland). Cultural and musical events are also held here, and there's a shop, gallery and information centre, where you can find out more about the city's Jewish heritage.

Plac Nowy

Until World War II, **Plac Nowy**, in the centre of Kazimierz and flanked by ul. Estery and ul. Warszauera, was the Jewish market. The ritual slaughterhouse rotunda at its centre recalls the area's former use. Nowadays, several of the best bars and cafés in Kraków are located here, attracting everyone from the area's colourful eccentrics to groups of youths feasting on kebabs.

East of the square, on ul. Kupa, is **Isaac Synagogue** (Synagoga Izaaka; open

Isaac Synagogue exhibition

New Jewish Cemetery

Mon–Sat 9am–7pm; admission fee), a 17th-century Judaic-Baroque masterpiece that was once famous for its stunning interior. Gutted by the Nazis, the synagogue is being restored to its former glory, but you can still come here and watch old films of Jewish life in the city before World War II.

North of Plac Nowy, at the junction of ul. Podbrzezie and ul. Miodowa, is the Reform (as opposed to Orthodox) Jewish congregation's **Tempel Synagogue** (Synagoga Templu; open Sun–Fri 10am–6pm; admission fee). Built in 1862, it was extended on both sides in 1924. It was one of the the very few synagogues in Kazimierz that survived the Nazi regime virtually intact. The façade combines neo-Renaissance with Moorish influences, while the interior is beautifully ornamented with ornate stucco work, intricate red-and-gold polychromy, and a set of four circular stained-glass windows by the altar closet.

New Jewish Cemetery

Established in 1800 as a replacement for the overflowing Remuh Cemetery, the 19-hectare (47-acre) **New Jewish Cemetery** (Nowy Cmentarz Żydowski; open Sun–Fri 10am–dusk), at the eastern end of ul. Miodowa (No. 55) beyond the railroad tracks, was the favoured place of burial for the well-off members of Kraków's Jewish community until the German invasion of the city in September 1939. The Nazis desecrated the cemetery, destroying most of the gravestones. Now partially restored, the cemetery is nevertheless overgrown. A few original gravestones remain, and fragments of broken headstones have been incorporated into the cemetery walls. There are also a number of memorials to entire families murdered during the Holocaust. A visit here is a haunting experience, and essential to anyone interested in Kraków's or Poland's Jewish history.

Two Museums

Apart from Jewish heritage and hedonistic hang-outs, Kazimierz also offers some other interesting attractions. The city's intriguing and informative **Ethnographic Museum** (Muzeum Etnograficzne; open Mon 10am–6pm, Wed–Fri 10am–3pm, Sat–Sun 10am–2pm; admission fee) is located inside what was once Kazimierz's Town Hall on pl. Wolnica, southwest of pl. Nowy. Due to celebrate its centenary in 2011, the museum was founded by the local teacher and folklore enthusiast Seweryn Udziela (1857–1937) as a way of preserving and promoting local folk culture within the region. Arranged over three floors, this extensive collection of folk art and culture from villages in the Kraków, Podhale and Silesian regions includes painted furniture, folk costumes and a small selection of the city's famous Christmas cribs *(see page 88)*. The top floor is given over entirely to a stunning collection of folk art, including paintings, paper cuttings and crude wooden sculptures.

Kazimierz's other notable museum, a couple of streets to the northeast at ul. św. Wawrzyńca 15, is the **City Engineering Museum** (Muzeum Inżynierii Miejskiej; open Tues–Sun 10am–4pm; admission fee). It's really two museums in one. The main part is a motor museum, a fascinating collection of old cars, motorcycles, trams and other motor vehicles.

Ethnographic Museum

Children especially will love the other part of the museum, the Fun and Science exhibition, which is located in a room adjoining the motor museum. This interactive hotchpotch of levers, pulleys and weights certainly lives up to its name. Some of the exhibits are decidedly whimsical, such as the cucumber that's had electrodes inserted into it; a voltameter proves that it generates an electric charge.

Catholic Kazimierz

There are several notable Catholic churches in the Kazimierz area. Of particular interest is the **Pauline Church** (Kościół Paulinów; ul. Skałeczna), located close to the river. The story of its founding is the stuff of legend: in 1079 or thereabouts the bishop of Kraków, Stanisław Szczepański, got himself into a bit of trouble with King Bolesław II the Bold, who accused him of treason and subsequently cut off his head. Shortly after this, Bolesław's family fell under a terrible curse, and to make amends for what was believed to be retribution for the decapitation and to appease the spirit of poor Stanisław, this magnificent building was constructed. Well worth having a peep inside, the church is also the final resting place of the city's creative genius, Stanisław Wyspiański. Bishop Szczepański was eventually canonised and is buried in Wawel Cathedral *(see page 44)*.

PODGÓRZE

Directly south of Kazimierz, across the Wisła, lies the sleepy suburb of Podgórze, with its rather run-down collection of local shops and dirty factories. Podgórze has one claim to fame: it was Kraków's ghetto during World War II. In 1941, between 3 and 21 March, the entire Jewish population of Kazimierz was marched across the Powstańców Sląskich bridge and into 320 houses in the area around today's pl. Bohaterów Getta. A 3m (10ft) wall was built around the new ghetto. Until its final liquidation on 13–14 March 1943, the ghetto was home to around 16,000 Jews, of whom almost all were either worked to death or murdered at the nearby concentration camp at Płaszów *(see page 58)* or at Auschwitz *(see page 70)*. Although there's not much to see, what remains is a poignant reminder of what the Nazis did in Poland between 1939 and 1944, and is worth taking the time to see.

Ghetto Heroes' Square

Take tram No. 9, 13, 32 or 34 south over the Wisła and get off at the first stop, **pl. Bohaterów Getta** (Ghetto Heroes' Square). The square and tram stop feature a sculpture consisting of 70 scattered upright chairs made of bronze. Designed by Piotr Lewicki and Kazimierz Łatak, and called *Nowy Plac Zgody* ('New Concordia Square', a reference to the square's former name, Concordia Square), the chairs are meant to recall a passage in a book by Tadeusz Pankiewicz *(see page 56)* describing the furniture left lying in the street after the ghetto's residents were rounded up for the final time in 1943. The monument is an

The Kraków ghetto's most famous survivor is the film director Roman Polański. He's been one of the main contributors to the promotion of Podgórze as part of Kraków's increasingly popular tourist trail.

interesting and for once non-controversial tribute to the terrible events that took place in this area.

In the far southwest corner of the square is the **Museum of National Remembrance** (Muzeum Pamięci Narodowej; open Tues–Thur 9.30am–4pm, Fri 10am–5pm, Sat 9.30am–4pm; admission fee). This was the site of the Pharmacy Under the Eagle (Apteka Pod Orłem), owned and run by Tadeusz Pankiewicz, the ghetto's only Gentile inhabitant *(see box below)*. The museum is a small affair, but it packs a powerful punch, featuring black-and-white photographs and some extraordinary films of ghetto life.

Heading further south along ul. Lwowska is the first of two surviving pieces of **ghetto wall**. About two-thirds of the way along on the right-hand side, this is the smaller of the two remaining sections, but is the more famous and is accordingly commemorated with a small plaque. The second and much larger piece that once marked the ghetto's southern edge is hidden away to the left and behind the secondary school at ul. Limanowskiego 13.

Tadeusz Pankiewicz

Tadeusz Pankiewicz (1908–93) was a Polish pharmacist and proprietor of the Apteka Pod Orłem (Pharmacy Under the Eagle) in Podgórze. In 1941 the Germans built the ghetto inside the area where his pharmacy was located. Declining an offer to relocate, he chose to live and work inside the ghetto along with his three Polish assistants. Besides his regular activities as a pharmacist, Pankiewicz gave sedatives to Jewish children to keep them quiet during Gestapo raids, and used his pharmacy as a secret meeting place for the ghetto's underground, as well as a place to hide Jews facing deportation to the death camps. After the war, Israel recognised him as Righteous Among the Nations, and he wrote a book, *The Kraków Ghetto Pharmacy*, about his experiences.

Schindler in his factory – a still from *Schindler's List*

Schindler's Kraków

Backtrack the way you just came and head slightly to the east to **Fabrika Oskara Schindlera** (ul. Lipowa 4). The extraordinary events that took place here are widely known thanks to the Steven Spielberg's film *Schindler's List*. Oskar Schindler (1908–74), from a wealthy and well-connected background, was born in the Czechoslovakian town of Svitavy. In 1930 he joined the Nazi Party and to avoid conscription moved to Kraków at the start of the war, where he bought a bankrupt enamel factory from its Jewish owner and staffed it with cheap Jewish labour. Thanks to his charm and ability to conjure up desirable black-market goods, Schindler soon won over the SS. He was able to set up a sub-camp of the neighbouring Płaszów concentration camp *(see page 58)* in the factory grounds, where his Jewish workers were able to live in relative peace.

In the summer of 1944 Schindler's workers were moved back to Płaszów, and it was at this time that he drew up his famous list of around 1,100 men and women working for him. He had them transferred to a weapons factory he established at his own cost in the town of Brünnlitz, close to where he was born. Three hundred Jewish women destined for Brünnlitz were accidentally sent to Auschwitz, and again Schindler used his connections to have them taken out (an act entirely unheard of in the Third Reich) and moved to the safety of Brünnlitz, where they were eventually liberated by the Red Army on 9 May 1945.

After an unsuccessful period in Argentina after the war, Schindler returned to Germany in 1958, and four years later was recognised by Israel as one of the Righteous Among the Nations. He died in Frankfurt in 1974, and was buried in a Christian cemetery on Mount Zion in Jerusalem. His acts of bravery were even more impressive given that Poland was the only German-occupied country during World War II where helping a Jew was punishable by death.

The factory itself is an unremarkable building. At the time of writing it was possible to watch films and visit a recreation of Schindler's office, but this is all set to change with the imminent renovation of the building.

Płaszów Concentration Camp

Płaszów concentration camp opened in 1942 just west of Podgórze, on the site of two Jewish cemeteries destroyed by the Nazis. Now overgrown and almost completely destroyed, it was originally designed as a work camp for German, Jewish and Polish workers. In its later incarnation, most prisoners were Jewish and Roma. Płaszów rose to notoriety at the beginning of 1943 when it was taken over by the sadistic camp commander Amon Goeth, an Austrian by birth who joined the Nazi Party as a keen young man of just 17. Shortly after Goeth's arrival, 6,300 residents of the Kraków ghetto were moved here, and the camp began its

In memory of those who died at Płaszów

harshest phase, when it became the scene of unspeakable cruelty. (Goeth is the character seen shooting children from his balcony in *Schindler's List.*) Public torture and execution were almost daily occurrences at Płaszów. Captured at war's end, an unrepentant Amon Goeth was tried, found guilty and hanged for his crimes on 13 September 1946.

Płaszów can be reached by taking tram No. 9, 13, 32 or 34 south a couple of stops from pl. Bohaterów Getta to Cmentarz Podgórski. Continue up the hill and take a right along ul. Jerozolimska. The camp entrance is by the second sign on the right. The main sights can be found at the top of the hill, up to the footpath on the left just after the cave. Of particular and startling interest is the Communist-built **monument**, dating from 1964, which commemorates all who died at the camp. Many of those who died at Płaszów were buried in the camp. Remember when you're here that what you're walking on is a mass grave site.

The district of Nowa Huta is named after the steelworks

NOWA HUTA

The vast working-class district of Nowa Huta (New Steelworks), some 10km (6 miles) east of the city centre, was constructed soon after the end of World War II as an industrial centre that would help rebuild a nation flattened by both the Germans and the Allies during the war's six years. The Lenin Steelworks was the main development. Over the years the population of the new district grew rapidly, and today about 100,000 people live in Nowa Huta.

Paid for by the Soviet Union, Nowa Huta was constructed in the monumental socialist-realist architectural style typical of the Communist era. The object of socialist realism was the veneration of the working class and its self-appointed leaders. Nowa Huta is the only complete socialist-realist town in the EU, and it's this architectural and political heritage that draws increasing numbers of visitors here. It's a tourist destination like no other.

Socialist-Realist Sights

Trams No. 4 and 15 take about 30 minutes from the centre of Kraków to **Plac Centralny**, the central square of Nowa Huta and the starting point of a socialist-realist trip to the district. The square has been officially renamed in honour of the former

US President Ronald Reagan. Built in 1949, it's surrounded by huge, ostentatious concrete buildings whose style supposedly echoes Poland's great Baroque and Renaissance architecture. Five streets radiate from the square, of which the middle one, al. Róż, leads to an area in the northwest featuring most of the interesting and representative socialist-realist buildings.

Just past the park on the right heading up al. Róż and located inside the **Tourist Information Centre** (os. Słoneczne 16) is the **Nowa Huta Museum** (Muzeum Narodowe Oddział Nowa Huta; open Tues–Sat 10am–4pm; admission fee), featuring temporary exhibits related to the area. The Tourist Information Centre provides free maps of Nowa Huta with all of the main sights indicated, but be warned: a number of the sights are marked in the wrong place.

Heading northwest is **Sfinks** (os. Górali 5; open Mon–Sat 9am–9pm, Sun 4.30pm–9pm), a combined cinema and cultural centre of the type once seen all over the Communist world and barely worth mentioning if it wasn't for the superb collection of abstract paintings by the avant-garde Kraków Group upstairs.

Nearby is the **Teatr Ludowy** (os. Teatralne 34; <www.ludowy.pl>). The People's Theatre was built in 1955 and looks like a cross between a seaside pavilion and a Roman palace. Famous countrywide for its experimental approach, the theatre once brought together groups of rival punks and skinheads to stage a production of *Romeo and Juliet*.

Southeast of Nowa Huta is the tiny settlement of Mogiła, which is home to a remarkable pair of churches found on either side of ul. Klasztorna. Huge 13th-century St Wenceslas church in the Cistercian Abbey features intricate folk-art motifs on its walls and ceiling, while across the street 15th-century St Bartholomew's is the only wooden church in Krakow.

Across the street and impossible to miss, thanks to the large tank parked outside, is the **Museum of the Armed Act** (os. Górali 23; Muzeum Czynu Zbrojnego; open Tues–Fri 10am–4pm; entrance by donation). It's a dark and dusty collection of memorabilia that celebrates Nowa Huta's military contributions to Polish history and the steelworkers who fought for their nation in battlefields all over the world. It contains photographs, uniforms and a disturbing series of models featuring scenes of Nazi atrocities and concentration-camp life.

Arka Pana Church

Head northwest along ul. Obroncow Krzyza to pl. B. Włosika where you will find Nowa Huta's **Arka Pana Church** (Kościół Arka Pana; open daily 6am–6.30pm). It was constructed between 1967 and 1977 with no assistance from the officially atheist Communist regime. Instead, local people built it using nothing but their bare hands and limited tools. The method of construction may have been basic, but Wojciech Pietrzyk's design, built to resemble Noah's Ark, is nothing short of breathtaking. Inside the two-level structure, the tabernacle includes a tiny fragment of rutile brought from the moon by the crew of Apollo 11, and one of the many sculptures, *Our Lady the Armoured*, was forged from 10kg (22lb) of shrapnel removed from Polish soldiers wounded at the World War II Battle of Monte Cassino, Italy. The imposing sculpture of Christ on the church's upper level breaks with convention, showing him blissfully flying to Heaven.

Head east through leafy socialist-realist residential streets to al. Solidarności, a long and stately road that leads from pl. Centralny to the entrance to the **Sendzimir** (formerly Lenin) **Steelworks**. On either side of the main gates are a pair of classic socialist-realist buildings known locally as the ***Doge*** after the Venetian palace they supposedly resemble. From here a No. 4 tram from the Kombinat stop runs back to the city centre.

Built by the locals, Arka Pana Church

OUTLYING SIGHTS

Like any other large city, Kraków wasn't planned with tourists in mind. Accordingly there are a number of recommended sights spiralling out from the centre and into the depths of the city's suburbs, although most of the places to visit listed below are within easy walking distance of the Old Town. The sights are divided into eastern and western areas. Visiting the places in either area can be done in a few hours if you take everything in, with the exception of the zoo in the west and the Aviation Museum way out of the city centre in the east. The latter is virtually in Nowa Huta, and is worth visiting as part of a trip there.

To the East

On the other side of the railway station is **Celestat** (ul. Lubicz 16; open Tues–Wed 11am–6pm, Thur 11am–6pm, Fri–Sat 9am–4pm; admission fee). Also known as the

On 9 June, in a traditional ceremony on the Rynek, the outgoing king of the Fowler Brotherhood presents the silver cockerel to the new incumbent.

History of Kraków's Marksmanship Guild, and by far the strangest museum in Kraków if not Poland, Celestat celebrates the history and culture of the city's **Fowler Brotherhood** (Bractwo Kurkowe), a peculiar bunch if ever there was one. The medieval Fowler Brotherhood was the Home Guard of its day. Brotherhoods all over Poland had the job of defending their respective cities. Made up of members of the merchant classes, the Fowler Brotherhood favoured the lavish oriental dress style of the Sarmatians *(see page 17)*, elected their own kings and, for reasons that nobody really understands, worshipped a silver cockerel. The Kraków Fowler Brotherhood, which is still very much alive and whose members can be found in attendance at major events in the city, used to crown new kings in St Mary's Basilica, an indication of its standing in the community.

The museum contains a fine range of exhibits, including paintings of former kings, the story of Fowler Brothers who perished at Auschwitz, and a 16th-century silver cockerel. Kraków's most famous Fowler Brother was a cunning gentleman by the name of Marcin Oracewicz, who, so the legend goes, while rushing to defend the city during the Confederation of Bar (1768–72) forgot to bring his bullets.

He therefore loaded his gun with his own buttons, of which one hit and mortally wounded the great Russian colonel, Panin. A small bust of Oracewicz stands outside the museum, and a plaque commemorating the shooting can be found on the east wall of the Barbican *(see page 34)*, the supposed scene of this heroic deed.

Botanical Gardens

A few minutes southeast of Celestat are the city's **Botanical Gardens** (Ogród Botaniczny Kraków; open Apr–Oct daily 9am–7pm; admission fee). Founded in 1783 by the Jagiellonian University, these are the oldest botanical gardens in Poland. Their 10 hectares (25 acres) include herb gardens, hothouses, ponds with water plants, a wonderfully fragrant collection of roses, as well as pleasant, tree-lined paths. A visit here makes a nice break from tramping the city's

In the Botanical Gardens

A Nazi aircraft in the Polish Aviation Museum

streets. The gardens also play host to a series of classical music concerts during the summer months.

Polish Aviation Museum

Out of the city centre just west of Nowa Huta is the **Polish Aviation Museum** (Muzeum Lotnictwa Polskiego; al. Jana Pawła II 39; open Mon–Fri 9am–5pm, Sat–Sun 10am–4pm; admission fee; <www.muzeumlotnictwa.pl>), a better than average collection of flying machines and other aeronautical memorabilia inside a couple of old hangars on a former airfield. Among the antique wooden machines and piles of rusty Soviet-era MIG fighters are a few things that really stand out, including one of the world's few remaining Spitfires in perfect condition. To get there take tram No. 4, 5 or 15 to the AWF stop, and walk back the way you came a short distance; the museum is behind some trees close to the extraordinary statue on the northern side of the road.

To the West

A 15-minute walk northwest of the Old Town along ul. Karmelicka takes you to Poland's only museum given over entirely to the art of photography, the **History of Photography Museum** (Muzeum Historii Fotografii; ul. Józefitów 16; open Wed–Fri 11am–6pm, Sat–Sun 10am–3.30pm; admission fee). Look past the museum's small size and uninspiring collection of old cameras to the permanent display of old pictures of the city. The museum also stages temporary exhibitions of every photographic style, sometimes of excellent quality.

A recommended short itinerary for those on foot after leaving the photography museum starts by heading south through the 5-hectare (12-acre) **Park Krakowski**, which was laid out in 1887 by Stanisław Rehman and was once the location of an outdoor theatre. Looking a little tatty these days, the park is scattered with a few interesting modern sculptures. There are other sculptures further down the street, outside the **University of Science and Technology** (Politechnika Krakowska; al. Mickiewicza 30). Ceramic figures of miners and steelworkers grace either side of the main entrance to the building. The work of Jan Raszka (1871–1945), they appear to be typically heroic characters from the days of Communism, but they actually predate that era, having been produced in 1935.

National Museum

Immediately to the south lies one of the highlights of the city if not Poland, the **National Museum** (Muzeum Narodowe; al. 3 Maja 1; open Nov–Apr Tues, Thur and Sun 10am–3pm, Wed and Fri–Sat 10am–6pm, May–Oct Tues and Thur 10am–4pm, Wed

To the west of the city centre is the Błonia, a lovely city park covering 120 hectares (296 acres) of meadow. It's particularly favoured by Kraków's dog-walking and jogging communities.

Display in the National Museum's Arms and Uniforms Gallery

and Fri–Sat 10am–7pm, Sun 10am–3pm; admission fee; <www.muz-nar.krakow.pl>). There are three galleries. Suits of armour, swords, firearms, medals and much more militaria are on display in the Arms and Uniforms Gallery. The Gallery of Decorative Art has a large collection of Polish and Western European decorative arts and crafts from medieval times to the early 1900s. The Gallery of 20th-century Polish Art contains over 400 works, and includes excellent coverage of the Young Poland (Młoda Polksa) art movement. The museum also hosts quality temporary exhibitions, and there's a good bookshop and a small café. It's close to the stop for the bus to the zoo *(see below)*, so you might want to consider visiting these two destinations in one trip.

Kraków Zoo

Much further out into the depths of Kraków's leafy suburbs is **Kraków Zoo and Zoological Gardens** (Miejski Park i Ogród Zoologiczny w Krakowie; ul. Kasy Oszczędności 14; open daily 9am–6pm; admission fee). You'll find the usual collection of big cats and frisky monkeys, as well as a small zoo made especially for children. The zoo is surrounded by the city's Zoological Gardens, a popular place for picnics away from the noise of the metropolis. To get there, take a westbound bus No. 134 from the stop just west of the National Museum. The journey time is about 20 minutes.

EXCURSIONS

Each of the following four destinations can be explored in a day. Two of these, Tarnów and Zakopane, also provide an opportunity to expand on a Kraków city break. Tarnów's immediate charm lies in its superb Old Town, but its other points of interest, including museums and a rich Jewish heritage, justify a longer visit if you have the time. The same can be said for Zakopane, with its rapidly expanding nightlife scene and year-round opportunities for outdoor activities in the magnificent Tatra Mountains.

Wieliczka Salt Mines

Twenty million years ago the area around Kraków was covered by sea. When the water receded, a large deposit of salt was left under the ground, which has been a source of

St Anthony's Chapel in the salt mines of Wieliczka

Since the middle of the 19th century, when salt baths were first touted for their healing potential, Wieliczka has also enjoyed the benefits of a sanatorium. Today the mines' underground chambers are still used as a location for the treatment of respiratory illnesses, particularly asthma, and allergies.

wealth in the region since the Stone Age. In the 13th century, large-scale rock salt extraction began, and mines sprang up (or rather, down) everywhere. The UNESCO-protected mines at **Wieliczka** (open daily 7.30am–7.30pm; admission fee; <www.kopalnia.pl>) are 10km (6 miles) southeast of Kraków, accessible by train from the main station or by minibus from ul. Grodzka in front of the Royal Hotel. There are nine levels, ranging from 64m (210ft) to 327m (1,075ft) down. Over the centuries, the numerous subterranean chambers have been carved and decorated by miners. Highlights include **St Anthony's Chapel**, created in the 17th century, and the mines' 23,000 cu m (812,200 cu ft) masterpiece, the **Chapel of St Kinga**, with beautiful carvings of New Testament scenes. Visits are by guided tour only, ending at a combined restaurant and gift shop before you rocket up to ground level in a lift.

Auschwitz

About 75km (47 miles) west of Kraków lies the small and seemingly insignificant town of **Oświęcim**, better-known to the world under its German name, **Auschwitz**. This was the site of two Nazi concentration camps, Auschwitz I and Auschwitz II (Birkenau). An estimated 1.1 million people died in the camps, and 90 percent of them were Jewish.

Auschwitz is by far the most popular day trip from Kraków. Each year, about half a million people make the journey here to try to comprehend the incomprehensible. Both camps are frightening, terrible and deeply disturbing places to visit. Think hard about what you're expecting to get from Auschwitz before you go there.

Auschwitz I (open 8am–7pm; free; <www.auschwitz.org.pl>) was the first camp to open, in 1940. Pass through the gates bearing the infamous maxim *Arbeit Macht Frei* ('Work Brings Freedom') and enter a place of unspeakable wickedness. Developed on the grounds of an abandoned Polish army camp, Auschwitz I remains almost intact, looking more like an old holiday resort than the site of some of the worst crimes ever committed. The red-brick barracks are dedicated to the nationalities who died here. Other sights include the wall where inmates were shot; a harrowing collection of suitcases, shoes, other personal possessions and even human hair; the (recreated) ovens where the dead were turned to ash; and, just next to the ovens, the gallows where camp commandant Rudolf Hoess was executed in 1947.

Railway leading to the entrance of Birkenau, or Auschwitz II

Three kilometres (2 miles) away lies the second camp, Auschwitz II, or **Birkenau**. Opened in 1941, Birkenau became the main site of the extermination of the Jewish race after the Final Solution was approved by the Germans in 1942. Trains from all over Europe could go right into the camp. On arrival, a selection of prisoners took place – three-quarters of all new arrivals were immediately taken away and murdered in the gas chambers. With little in the way of exhibits, Birkenau somehow captures the sheer terror of Auschwitz more than the original camp.

Getting to Auschwitz is easy, with plenty of buses leaving from the main bus station each day, and there are also a few trains. Tours from Kraków are plentiful, and are worth considering, although prices tend to be high. People visiting Auschwitz independently should buy the excellent brochure from the small kiosk on the right as you enter the main doors of Auschwitz I.

Tarnów

Located 80km (50 miles) to the east of Kraków, the small town of **Tarnów** boasts an almost perfectly preserved Old Town of impressive Gothic, Baroque and Renaissance architecture. Scratch the surface and you'll also find reminders of a rich history involving Jews, Roma and many others. The town is just one hour from Kraków by express train, and the best bits can be seen comfortably in a day if you get up early. However, there are plenty of attractions to warrant an overnight stay.

Rynek and the Old Town

Tarnów's Old Town retains its original layout of a raised central area of latticed streets with a grand market square (Rynek) at its centre and a lower, oval-shaped encompassing loop reached by a series of stairways. The Old Town began

Colourful merchant houses in Tarnów's Rynek

life in the 14th century, although most of what now stands dates from later periods. With its magnificent merchant houses, fine museums and other notable sights, the Old Town should be your first port of call.

The Old Town's crowning glory is the **Rynek**, a wide-open plaza surrounded by fine Renaissance houses. The Rynek's centrepiece is the 15th-century **Town Hall** (Ratusz), an elaborate yellow Gothic and Renaissance building with attics topping its roof and a 30m (100ft) tower. Inside is the **Tarnów District Museum** (Muzeum Okręgowe w Tarnowie; open Tues 10am–5pm, Wed–Fri 9am–5pm, Sat–Sun 10am–2pm; admission fee). Among the highlights are Poland's best collection of 18th-century Sarmatian portraits *(see page 17)* and a celebration of the life of the soldier and patriot Józef Bem (1794–1850), who was born in Tarnów. A smaller branch of the museum at **nos 20–21** (same opening hours as main museum; admission fee) puts on temporary displays. During the summer, the Rynek comes alive with outdoor cafés, and is a great place to sit and socialise.

In the northeast corner of the Rynek is the **cathedral** (katedra; open 6am–6.30pm). Dating from the 14th century, with later additions made in the 15th and 19th centuries, the now mostly neo-Baroque red-brick building has a number of points of interest, both inside and out. Of particular note are the fine 16th-century monuments to the Tarnowski family, who once owned the town, and the 72m (236ft) high tower, visible throughout the town and forming a useful landmark. Immediately behind the Cathedral is the **Diocesan Museum** (Muzeum Diecezjalne; open Tues–Fri 10am–3pm, Sat 9am–2pm, Sun 10am–3pm; free), which has a collection of religious art from the 15th century onwards.

Tarnów's cathedral

Jewish Tarnów

Directly east of the Rynek in a part of the Old Town now populated by a number of interesting little bars and Tarnów's exceptional Roma restaurant Ke Maro *(see page 141)* is the area where the majority of the town's Jews lived, until the Holocaust obliterated a people that from the 15th century until June 1944 made up around 40 percent of Tarnów's population.

The part of the Old Town between ul. Żydowska and ul. Wekslarska still features

At its height, Tarnów's Jewry was a thriving secular and religious community of both Orthodox and Hasidic Jews, many of whom held distinguished positions in the town. Sadly, the largest reminder of Jewish life today is the massive Jewish graveyard at the junction of ul. Słoneczna and ul. Matki Bożej Fatimskie.

a handful of Jewish houses with their original *mezuzah* boxes in the doorways – a haunting reminder of what used to be. Heading east along ul. Żydowska on the left is a massive, forlorn-looking ***bimah***, all that's left of the town's 17th-century synagogue after the Nazis burnt it down on the evening of 9 November 1939. Heading further in the same direction out of the Old Town, at pl. Bohaterów Getta, is the 1904 **Moorish Jewish Bath House**, now a gruesome footnote in the town's history – it was the site of the first Nazi deportation, of 728 people, five of them Jews, to Auschwitz.

Other Highlights

There are a number of exceptional sights within easy walking distance of the Old Town. Between the railway station and the Old Town at ul. Krakowska 10 is the **Ethnographic Museum** (Muzeum Etnograficzne; open Tues, Thur 10am–5pm, Wed, Fri 9am–3pm, Sat–Sun 10am–2pm; admission fee), inside a gorgeous wooden cottage. It's crammed with colourful folk costumes and art from the region, as well as what's claimed to be the only permanent display on Roma culture in Europe. The Roma (Gypsies) have been living in Tarnów since the 15th century and are still represented by around 200 individuals, including the charming family of musicians who run the restaurant mentioned above. The museum is well worth a visit, especially if you pay a little extra for Adam Bartosz's excellent book *The Gypsies*, which includes a concise yet thorough history of Roma life and culture in the region.

In the south, not too far from one another, are two fine wooden churches. Closest to the centre on ul. Panny Marii is **St Mary's Church** (Kościół Najświętszej Marii Panny). This diminutive 15th-century larch building is often open, rewarding visitors with a glimpse inside a typical Polish parish church, typified by colourful painted flowers on the ceiling. A little further south on ul. Tuchowska is the **Holy Trinity Church** (Kościół św. Trójcy), a 16th-century Gothic building notable for the painting *Throne of Grace*, depicting God with six fingers on his left hand, signifying the number of days taken to create the Earth.

Additional information about Tarnów can be found by visiting the excellent official tourist information website: <www.it.tarnow.pl>.

A bucolic scene near the Tatras

The Tatras

Traditional Zakopane costume

The highest section of the Carpathian mountain range, the Tatras cover an area that takes in the region immediately south of Zakopane and stretching into neighbouring Slovakia. The spectacular karst peaks, dense pine forests and clear lakes make up one of the few areas of pristine wilderness in Europe, where eagles fly and brown bears and chamois roam. The Tatras are a hugely popular summertime destination for Polish hikers, while in the winter, skiers come to enjoy the slopes dotted around Zakopane and take the cable car to the 1,000m (3,300ft) runs on the Kasprowy Wierch mountain.

Inside a small hut next to the Rondo Kuźnickie is the **Tatra National Park Information Centre** (ul. Chałubińskiego 42a; open daily 7am–3pm; tel: 018 202 32 88; <www.tpn.pl>), where you'll find more information on things to see and do in the Tatras. They also sell maps and guidebooks in English.

Zakopane

Nestled in the dip of a valley between the hillside hamlet of Gubałówka and the northernmost tip of the Tatra Mountains, the small wooden town of **Zakopane** is renowned throughout Poland as both the nation's winter capital and as a place to come for rest and relaxation. It was originally a village of the Gorals (Górale), a small ethnic group of mountain people, and became a popular destination thanks to the tireless promotion of 19th-century doctor Tytus Chałubinski. Just

The Willa Koliba houses the Zakopane Style Museum

100km (62 miles) south of Kraków, Zakopane and its Goral culture makes for an interesting day trip at any time of year, and provides a more substantial base for those looking for adventures in the great outdoors.

A 10-minute walk south-west from the railway and bus stations along ul. Kościuszki brings you to the town's main street, **ul. Krupówki**. All three main sights can be found by turning right at this junction. Down the hill on the left at ul. Krupówki 10 is the **Tatra Museum** (Muzeum Tatrzańskie; open Wed–Sat 9am–4.30pm, Sun 9am–3pm; admission fee), where you can find out more about the region and its mountain culture. Housed inside a classic wooden house, the museum is spread over two floors. Exhibits include traditional costumes, old farming implements and recreations of the interiors of local homes as they were in the 19th century. Unfortunately, there's not a lot of information in English.

Turn left at the end of the street and just on the right is the charming and diminutive **St Mary of Częstochowa Church** (Kościół Matki Boskiej Częstochowskiej; open daily 9.30am–6pm). It was built entirely of wood between 1847 and 1851, and is Zakopane's oldest standing house of worship. The interior is decorated with folk art, but the church is perhaps more famous for its graveyard. This is the final resting place of the great and the good of the town, including Helena Marusarzówna *(see below)*, a former Polish skiing champion and resistance activist executed by the Nazis during World War II.

A little further up on the same side of the road is the town's first building in the wooden Zakopane Style. The **Zakopane Style Museum** (Muzeum Stylu Zakopiańskiego; open Wed–Sat 9am–4pm, Sun 9am–3pm; admission fee) is located inside the Willa Koliba, built in 1894 by Stanisław Witkiewicz and featuring rooms set out as they were when the building was constructed. At the top of the stairs are some fine carved wooden pieces in an almost Art Deco style, plus a large collection of paintings by Witkiewicz's son, known to the world as Witkacy (1885–1939), all painted under the influence of different drugs (the drug in question being recorded on each canvas along with the signature), and collectively far more infamous than they are accomplished.

Helena Marusarzówna

Of the many Polish World War II heroines, perhaps none is more deserving of remembrance than Helena Marusarzówna. Born in Zakopane in 1918, the year Poland regained its independence, the teenage mountain girl won seven Polish skiing championships between 1936 and the outbreak of World War II. Barely into her twenties, she joined the Polish underground and began smuggling mail and refugees over the Tatra Mountains and into Hungary. In March 1940, she was captured by the Hungarian police and handed over to the Gestapo, who tortured her on several occasions before they executed her the following year. She didn't give away a single secret, and was posthumously awarded the Virtuti Militari and the Cross of Bravery. She is buried in the graveyard of St Mary of Częstochowa Church.

WHAT TO DO

ENTERTAINMENT

With numerous theatres, music venues, cinemas, bars, clubs and festivals catering to every taste imaginable, Poland's unofficial cultural capital has an enormous capacity to keep its visitors entertained. The excellent **Cultural Information Centre** (open Mon–Sat 10am–6pm; ul. św. Jana 2; tel: 012 421 77 87) is full of information about cultural and entertainment events throughout the city. Tickets for a night at the opera or cinema cost as little as 15zł.

Theatre

Theatre performances are almost always in Polish, so check to see if simultaneous translations are available. The **Stary Teatr** (ul. Jagiellońska 5; tel: 012 422 85 66; <www.stary-teatr.pl>) was Poland's first ever playhouse. It focuses mostly on classic and lavish theatre productions from Poland and abroad. Other theatres of note include the **Bagatela** (ul. Karmelicka 6; tel: 012 422 26 44; <www.bagatela.krakow.pl>), Kraków's leading home of musical theatre and light entertainment; the fabulous **Juliusz Słowacki Theatre** (pl. św. Ducha 1; tel: 012 422 40 22; <www.slowacki.krakow.pl>), which prides itself on both grand theatre and the occasional opera *(see page 31)*; and the **Groteska Puppet, Mask & Actor Theatre** (ul. Skarbowa 2; tel: 012 633 96 04; <www.groteska.pl>), which preserves the very best traditions in Eastern European puppet and experimental theatre for both children and adults. Also worth a mention is Nowa Huta's typically offbeat, working-class **Teatr Ludowy** *(see page 61)*.

Kraków has a glowing bar scene

Classical and Opera

Especially during the summer, when many orchestras take to the streets and parks of the city, Kraków comes alive with classical concerts, opera and, particularly in the city's many churches, choral music.

The **Kraków Filharmonia** (ul. Zwierzyniecka 1; tel: 012 422 94 77; <www.filharmonia.krakow.pl>) is located just west of the Old Town in a rather ugly-looking building that belies what takes place inside. With no really great Polish symphonic heroes, the repertoire leans in the direction of the great German composers, although other music is played here.

The **Opera Krakówska** (ul. Lubicz 48; tel: 012 628 91 13; <www.opera.krakow.pl>) concentrates on the production of ostentatious opera classics. Kazimierz's smaller and less well-known **Kraków Opera Kameralna** (ul. Miodowa 15; tel: 012 430 66 06; <www.kok.art.pl) is the place to head for if you're looking to see some traditional Jewish theatre, including evenings of extraordinary Yiddish songs, as well as more Polish-orientated works.

Flower Etiquette

Giving flowers (*kwiaty*) in Poland comes with a sophisticated set of rules that if not followed can lead to potentially embarrassing situations, especially among the older generation. The most important things to know are that you should always give an odd number of flowers (even numbers are reserved for solemn occasions) and that they should be given with the left hand. You should give your fiancée red flowers, her mother pink, and stay clear of anything yellow, the traditional colour of envy. Chrysanthemums are for funerals only. Last but not least, carnations represent communism, so be careful who you give these to.

Juliusz Słowacki Theatre stages grand theatre and opera

Cinema

Poland has an enviable cinematic tradition, and the Poles are dedicated movie-goers. Three cinemas that are all worth attending for their individual merits are **ARS** (ul. św. Jana 6; tel: 012 421 41 99; <www.ars.pl>) in the Old Town, which caters to a mostly mainstream audience; **Kino Pod Baranami** (Rynek Główny 27; tel: 012 423 07 68; <www.kinopodbaranami.pl>), a fine cinema keeping the arthouse and independent cinema scene in the city alive as well as being the home of the annual Independent Film Festival in November; and the immense **IMAX** (al. Pokoju 44; tel: 012 290 90 90; <www.kinoimax.pl/krakow>), east of the city centre and reached on trams No. 1, 14 and 22. Galeria Kazimierz *(see also page 89)* also has a fine multiplex, **Cinema City**, catering to the needs of the average popcorn-fuelled, cinema-going public. All films are shown in their original language with Polish subtitles.

Jazz is popular on the bar circuit

Nightlife

Poland's best nightlife city, Kraków has a fine choice of bars, clubs and live music venues. The fact that the city centre is so small makes pub-crawling particularly attractive, especially when there appears to be a kebab shop between every drinking hole. Two cultural differences worth noting are that a Polish cocktail bar is in fact an ice-cream parlour (there are real cocktail bars too, but they're usually just called bars), and, particularly in the areas just outside the Old Town, many places that call themselves nightclubs are in fact brothels. A red light usually gives the game away.

Bars

Kazimierz has by far the finest selection of bars, with **Alchemia** (ul. Estery 5; tel: 012 421 22 00), a dark and gloomy affair, being the most talked about. Complete with a theatre and a cinema, service is at the bar, and is painfully slow.

Across the street, **Les Couleurs** (ul. Estery 10; tel: 012 429 42 70) is beautifully scruffy, has lots of meaningful posters on the walls to complement the meaningful clientele, and is highly recommended if you don't mind inhaling a year's worth of cigarette smoke in a single evening. Almost next door is **Singer** (ul. Estery 22; tel: 012 292 06 22). In a nutshell, Singer is superb, from the tables fashioned from old sewing machine stands (hence the name) to the sheer diversity of people who come here to drink. One bar worth seeking out in the Old Town is **Piękny Pies** (ul. św. Jana 18; tel: 012 421 45 52). Loud and raucous, it attracts a predominantly twentysomething crowd out for a good time before they head off to one of the many nightspots in the area.

During the balmy summer months, many of the hidden courtyards in the Old Town get clogged with chattering tables full of people out for a little alfresco boozing, creating one of the most pleasant and relaxed drinking experiences in the city. **Budda Drink & Garden** (Rynek Główny 6; tel: 012 421 65 22) is a compact, two-floor bar full of good-looking people; it's also painfully loud. The terrace here is a great place to guzzle beer and watch the world drift slowly by. Also worth a mention is **Tajemniczy Ogród** (ul. Bracka 3–5; tel: 012 429 38 14), which has an excellent shared courtyard.

Nic Nowego (ul. św. Krzyża 15; tel: 012 421 61 88) is a fine Irish-run glitzy sports bar serving good food and the best Guinness in southern Poland. **Someplace Else** (ul. Powiśle 7;

Kazimierz is a good place to seek one of these

tel: 012 662 10 00) is inside the Sheraton Hotel, so expect a Western bill at the end of a session. If that doesn't put you off, you'll be rewarded with a multitude of sports screens, supermodels behind the bar and a decent menu of snacks and light meals.

Clubs

Kraków's nightlife tempts everyone from lecherous stag parties to septuagenarian ladies out for a few shots of vodka and a good old knees-up. **Art Club Błędne Koło** (ul. Bracka 4; tel: 012 431 20 52) caters to people who look like they fell out of a fashion magazine, so dress nicely and they may well let you in.

At the other end of the scale, **Black Gallery** (ul. Mikołajska 24; tel: 012 423 00 30) would put an East Berlin punk bar to shame. Dark and dirty, this place is hugely popular with the city's more anarchic types.

Cień (ul. św. Jana 15; tel: 012 422 21 77) has more face control than a gurning convention and is packed with B-list beauties. Cień guarantees a good night out and the chance to mix with people who drive very expensive black cars.

A current stag favourite is **Prozak** (pl. Dominikański 6; tel: 012 429 11 28), whose policy involves keeping most Polish males away so the foreign lads can better enjoy the local talent. The drinks here are overpriced.

For a very gay old time indeed, **Kitsch** (ul. Wielopole 15/4; tel: 012 422 52 99) caters primarily but not exclusively to Kraków's gay and fetish community. A night here is generally a night to remember. Vast and amusing, this is an ideal place for hedonistic adventures.

For a thorough and up-to-date investigation of the city's nightlife, pick up a copy of *Kraków In Your Pocket* *(see page 119)* when you're in town.

The Cloth Hall has been a centre of commerce since medieval times

SHOPPING

Kraków offers a disparate mix of retail options, ranging from vast new shopping malls to shops selling religious souvenirs or 1960s bric-a-brac. The main shopping areas are the Old Town, given over almost exclusively to the sale of expensive designer clothes and cheap souvenirs, and Kazimierz, which is making a name for itself as the place to go for antiques and second-hand bargains.

Speciality Shopping

The area in and around the Rynek provides ample opportunities for picking up souvenirs, including amber, stuffed Wawel dragons, huge pencils and many other dubious treats. As well as selling this sort of thing, the ground floor of the **Cloth Hall** *(see page 27)* has some authentic and quite lovely local linen and folk art, including carved wooden sculptures of religious and agricultural scenes, and Góral leatherwear and knitwear.

The area running north–south east of the Rynek is the best place to pick up such things as flashing Jesus paintings, priests' outfits, holy wine and more. The quirky **Arkos** (pl. Mariacki 5; tel: 012 421 86 61; open Mon–Fri 10am–6pm, Sat 10am–2pm) is perhaps the most representative of these shops.

Local arts and crafts make excellent gifts and souvenirs, but it can be difficult to know what's what and whether you're getting the real thing. The excellent booklet ***Polish Folk Culture*** provides background to traditional arts and crafts, and makes a good souvenir in itself. It's also a guide to the Ethnographic Museum *(see page 53)*, and is sold there for 10zł.

Amber is the country's national stone, and jewellery made from either amber or silver, or both, often represents very good value. Try **Mikołajczyki Amber** (tel: 012 430 24 01; open Mon–Sat 9am–9pm, Sun 9am–8pm), in the Cloth Hall and other locations around the city.

If you're thinking of buying antiques, keep in mind that it's illegal to export items produced before 1945 – unless you elicit prior written permission from the government.

Christmas Cribs

Christmas cribs *(szopka)* are a speciality of Kraków. They began appearing in the 19th century, the work of local craftsmen with time on their hands during the slow autumn months. Large (often 2m/6.5ft), brightly coloured and ornately decorated portable theatres depicting the Nativity scene, these unique creations have become one of the symbols of the city. In 1937 the first competition was held in the city to choose the best, an event that continues to this day. During the morning of the first Tuesday of December, the best Christmas cribs are displayed in the Rynek between the Cloth Hall and St Mary's. The winners are later taken to the Ethnographic Museum in Kazimierz *(see page 53)*; the rest are sold on the spot.

Markets and Malls

Traditional lacemaking

Kraków's markets range from the sublime to the ridiculous. The former is represented by the wonderful **Kazimierz Market** (Plac Nowy; open daily 5.30am–3pm), which offers a rotating range of things to buy, from tacky clothing to the superb bric-a-brac market held every Saturday. The two central markets, selling cheap Chinese imports as well as a good choice of local cheese, meat and flowers, are the **Hala Turgowa** (Plac Targowy; hall open daily 6am–10pm; outdoor market Mon–Sat 6am–7pm, Sun 6am–2pm), which also sells a few second-hand goodies in the upstairs section of the hall, and **Stary Kleparz** (Rynek Kleparski; open Mon–Sat 6am–6pm), which has been in business for hundreds of years and is another source of flowers, sausages and local mushrooms during the autumn.

Malls are sprouting up everywhere and are a welcome sight during the harsh winter months especially. They have the usual clothing stores, electrical outlets, mobile phone shops, cafés and restaurants. The two heavyweights are **Galeria Kazimierz** (ul. Podgórska 34; open Mon–Sat 10am–10pm, Sun 10am–8pm), and **Galeria Krakowska** (ul. Pawia 5; open Mon–Sat 9am–10pm, Sun 10am–9pm), next to the railway station.

SPORTS AND ACTIVITIES

Swimming. The city has two excellent places in which to swim. **Park Wodny** (ul. Dobrego Pasterza 126; tel: 012 616 31 90; <www.parkwodny.pl>) is a massive complex with water slides as well as beauty facilities and a decent café. The smaller **Klub Sportowy Korona** (ul. Kalwaryjska 9–15; tel: 012 656 02 50; <www.korona.krakow.pl>) has a 25m (82ft) pool.

Ice-skating. The two ice rinks at **Lodowisko Krakowianka** (ul. Siedleckiego 7; tel: 012 421 13 17) are open to the public when the local ice-hockey team isn't using them.

Paintballing. With Kraków's blossoming as a top stag party destination, visitors to the city can now enjoy running about in a forest and shooting each other with coloured paint courtesy of a number of specialist companies, of which **Compass** (<www.compass-poland.com>) is consid-

Skiing on Kasprowy Wierch mountain in the Tatras

ered to be the most professional. Compass also organises many other puerile pursuits, including off-roading and the inevitable groom kidnappings.

Golf. Golf is available at two courses. The **Kraków Valley Golf & Country Club** (ul. Krzeszowice 3, Paczółtowice; tel: 012 282 94 67; <www.krakow-valley.com>) offers 18 holes some 40km (25 miles) west of the city, while in the opposite direction the posher **Royal Kraków Golf & Country Club** (ul. Ochmanów 124, Podłęże; tel: 012 281 91 70; <www.krakowgolf.pl>) provides nine holes 18km (11 miles) away in the splendid Royal Jagiellonian Hunting Grounds.

Hiking. The vast countryside of Poland is ideal for leisurely walking and more athletic hiking. One of the best areas for both, especially for serious hikers, are the High Tatra Mountains around Zakopane *(see page 77)*.

Skiing. Winter sports equipment is available in abundance in Zakopane, both for sale and hire, especially in the main street, ul. Krupówki. Ski rental costs from between about 35zł and 65zł per day. Renting a snowboard costs about 50zł a day. One hour with a ski instructor costs anything from 60zł up.

Football. Kraków's two professional football teams are **Cracovia** (ul. Kałuży 1; <www.cracovia.pl>) and **Wisła** (ul. Reymonta 22; <www.wisla.krakow.pl>). Both teams play in the country's top league. Be warned: Polish football crowds can get rough at times.

FESTIVALS

Kraków has a reputation as a city of great festivals. Among the outstanding events are May's international **Krakow Film Festival** (<www.cracowfilmfestival.pl>); the colossal **Jewish Festival of Culture** (<www.jewishfestival.pl>), held in Kazimierz and the Old Town each July; September's delightfully different **Sausage Dog Parade** (in which hundreds of owners of the diminutive beasts dress them up as pirates, pop stars and other creations before marching them around the Old Town); and the ancient pagan tradition of **Wianki** on St John's Day (24 June), when the young ladies of the city float candlelit wreaths down the Wisła River near Wawel, light bonfires and of course drink lots of alcohol. Then there are **classical concerts** inside the nearby salt mines in Wieliczka, an annual celebration of the music of **Bach**, a superb **jazz festival** and much more than space here allows. For more information about the city's festivals as well as one-off events, see <www.biurofestiwalowe.pl> or pick up a copy of the monthly magazine *Karnet*, available in hotels and kiosks around the city for 4zł.

CHILDREN'S KRAKÓW

Bringing your kids to Kraków is highly recommended just so long as you're prepared to put up with the occasional moment of hardship, such as most restaurants' lack of high chairs, children's menus and bite-size cutlery. Many sights cater for both small and big people, including Kazimierz's **City Engineering Museum** *(see page 53)*, which has a small hands-on section for children; **Kraków Zoo** *(see page 68)*, with its kids' area; and the water slides at **Park Wodny** *(see page 90)*. There is a large outdoor adventure playground in **H. Jordana Park** immediately northwest of the National Museum and an indoor playground inside **Galeria Kazimierz** *(see page 89)*. See the Kraków section of <www.inyourpocket.com> for a list of activities for children.

Tucking into some candy floss on the market square

Calendar of Events

Early January New Year classical concert deep inside the salt mines in Wieliczka *(see page 69)*, just east of the city.

March *Bach Days:* a series of concerts celebrating the music of the composer Johann Sebastian Bach. *Jazz in Kraków:* seven days of Polish and international jazz.

May *Great Dragon Parade:* in honour of the city's mythical fire-breathing dragon, including firework displays and huge flying dragons. *Museum Night:* for one night only, this is a fabulous way to enjoy the city's museums *(see page 25)*. *Soup Festival:* soup freaks converge on Kazimierz for a day of tasting soup in its many varieties; prizes are given in the evening for the best of the bunch. *Kraków Film Festival:* Poland's oldest film festival; films of every persuasion are shown, from home and abroad. *Kraków Marathon:* setting off from the Błonia (west of the city centre), the city's annual marathon goes all the way out to Nowa Huta, then snakes through the Old Town before getting back to where it all started.

June–August *Kraków Opera Summer:* opera concerts take place throughout the city, including a series of outdoor events inside the grounds of the Barbican.

9 June The coronation of the king of the Kraków Fowler Brotherhood takes place on the Rynek.

24 June *Wianki:* harking back to pagan days, this is a night festival of fire and feisty girls for all the family along the Wisła next to Wawel.

July *International Street Theatre Festival:* jugglers, fire-eaters and much absurdity and experimental theatre over three days in the Rynek.

Late July *Jewish Festival of Culture:* 10 days of everything Jewish, from Yiddish language courses and Yiddish theatre to kosher cooking and live *klezmer* music – staged in various venues and outdoors throughout Kazimierz and the Old Town.

September *Sausage Dog Parade:* the daft day of the dachshunds and their proud, albeit rather strange, owners.

November–January *Christmas Market:* the Rynek stages a market, with stalls of hot soup, Christmas gifts, colourful lights and concerts.

EATING OUT

It's true what they say about Polish food, more or less: there's an awful lot of cabbage out there, especially if you're eating in one of the country's less salubrious restaurants. But thankfully that's not the end of the story. The Poles are fanatical meat-eaters, and especially in the south, where there's a healthy Goral influence, they make an extremely good job of cooking it. A classic Polish meal is something such as soup with lashings of white and/or rye bread to start, followed by a meat-friendly main course of pork or chicken accompanied by the ubiquitous potato (more often than not now served in the form of crinkle-cut chips) and vegetables, which are often served raw and will almost certainly comprise of at least a little cabbage. Meals are finished off with a range of

Meat will be on the menu in your typical *restauracja*

desserts at which the Poles excel both in their preparation and consumption.

Restaurants

Many restaurants are located in historic buildings

Kraków's restaurant scene is currently expanding like a runaway soufflé, with new and more interesting places opening almost daily. The vast majority of restaurants are concentrated in the Old Town, and offer everything from classic *pierogi* to poppadoms. The Old Town is also by far the most expensive place to eat in the city. Kazimierz is primarily the nerve centre of the city's drinking culture, but does also boast the prime Jewish restaurants as well as the best Indian food in Kraków. As you venture outwards from the centre, the choices becomes less exciting, but again there are one or two exceptions to the rule.

As well as having every conceivable type of Polish cuisine, the city plays host to a plethora of international options, from kebabs to pizza (a Polish institution) to sushi. Many kitchens are now run by experienced chefs from abroad. While Poland is by no means known for vegetarian cuisine, the attitude is slowly changing. Meat-free options include Green Way *(see page 135)* and Momo *(see page 139).*

Menus in English are available in most places, and waiting staff in all but the lowliest of city-centre restaurants speak English, and quite often German as well. Much the same as the city's bars, many restaurants set up tables and chairs outdoors during the summer.

When to Eat

Breakfast *(śniadanie)* is usually eaten between 7am and 10am. Poles, including the inhabitants of Kraków, favour a cold breakfast, typically of bread, cheese, ham and a little salad. Hot breakfast, including an omelette, is gaining popularity and will be found on all but the cheapest hotel breakfast menus. Hotel breakfasts in general are undergoing a much-needed overhaul, with cold buffets being replaced with a more international style. Tea is taken without milk.

Lunch *(obiad)* starts from as early as 11am and can go on until somewhere around 3pm. Business lunches are becoming more and more popular. Dishes are basic, with a three-course meal made up of a simple soup with plenty of white or rye bread, a main course consisting of usually meat and plenty of cabbage, and a simple dessert. Alcohol is generally not drunk during lunch.

Fried meat stall in the market square

Dinner *(kolacja)* is eaten between 6pm and 9pm. Meals tend to be similar to those eaten at lunchtime. Poland is a nation of traditionalists, and dinnertime remains a home-based family affair. As Western standards continue to influence Polish culture, going out for dinner is becoming more popular.

***Barszcz* – beetroot soup**

Meat, Fish and Vegetarian Options

For most Poles a meal of substance includes meat. Pork is by far the most popular meat dish. The classic preparation is a pork cutlet prepared with fried onions, coated in breadcrumbs and served with stewed cabbage. Roast pork is eaten both hot and cold. Hot pot roast may be served with dried prunes. Beef is less common, though *zrazy zawijane* (beef rolls filled with bacon, dark bread and mushrooms) is a standard dish. The meat dish not to be missed is *bigos* *(see page 98)*.

Game is very popular, as you might expect from the national affinity for meat and rich tastes. Venison *(sarna)* is usually reserved for elite restaurants, as are wild boar *(dzik)* and other 'exotic' game. Look, too, for hare *(zając)* and pheasant *(bażant)*. Chicken *(kurczak)* is common and not expensive. Polish chicken is typically stuffed and roasted. Chicken soup is another great Polish favourite, as is roasted duck *(kaczka)* with apples.

Fish is as popular on menus as pork and other meats. Pike, eel, perch, sturgeon and others – boiled, fried or roasted – are found in most good restaurants. Carp is a particular favourite (especially on Christmas Eve), often served in aspic or Polish sauce with raisins and almonds.

Vegetarians should steer towards potato pancakes or dumplings stuffed with fruit, *kopytka* (gnocchi), *pierogi* filled with cheese and potato, and crêpes. Salads include tomato salads, sliced cucumbers in sour cream, and sauerkraut.

An A–Z of Dishes

You will be bumping into the following dishes on menus more or less everywhere you go.

Bigos is a simple dish of sauerkraut with onions, meat and/or sliced sausage and occasionally mushrooms, simmered for hours and eaten on its own. The quality can vary from delicious to inedible.

A plate of *pierogi*

Gołąbki ('pigeons') are cabbage leaves stuffed with minced beef, onions and rice. They taste a lot better than they sound.

Made with anything from beef to turkey to bison, *kiełbasa* (Polish sausages) are usually excellent. *Krakowska* is a traditional local sausage with pepper and garlic.

The undisputed Polish folk dish is *pierogi*, small dough parcels filled with anything from minced pork or beef to cabbage or potato to sweet berries, and served with sour cream.

Placki are made by grating a potato to a pulp, mixing it with flour and egg, and then frying the result. Again, they are served with lashings of sour cream.

Smalec is, in a word, lard. It's delicious when served traditionally with fresh bread and a glass of beer.

Zapiekanki is Polish pizza. For sale in every underpass in the nation, *zapiekanki* is essentially a sliced baguette covered with mushrooms and melted cheese, smothered with tomato ketchup, and eaten while walking.

Oscypek **– smoked cheeses with folk patterns**

Zupa (soup) comes at the end of this list but the beginning of the meal. The two most common ones are *żurek*, a hot and, if well-made, thick, sour rye soup with sausages and potatoes, and *barszcz*, a thin beetroot soup often served with dumplings.

Local Specialities

The *precel* is a fabulously doughy white bread roll in the shape of a bagel, often sprinkled with seeds including poppy and sesame. Available for about 1zł, precels are sold from little barrows set up on every street corner in the city.

Originating in the Tatras, but for sale from seemingly every old lady's basket in Kraków, *oscypek* are spindle-shaped cheeses covered in elaborate folk patterns. Made traditionally from goats' cheese, *oscypek* are smoked, have a texture somewhere between a hard and soft cheese, and come in bite-sized versions as well as the classic size and occasional monster. A typical *oscypek* costs about 10zł. Many stalls can be found in Zakopane selling hot *oscypek* straight from a barbecue grill, on which you'll also find the main ingredient in the local Goral food, big hunks of roasting mutton from the nearby mountains.

Leave some room for cream cake

Sweets

Two things to look out for are the sublime *kremówka*, cream cakes that come in all manner of gooey and sickly varieties, and the home-grown Wawel chocolate, available in simple bars and fancy tins; there's even a magnificent 90 percent cocoa variety. They make excellent gifts and souvenirs. The Wawel Shop (Rynek Główny 33; tel: 012 423 12 43; <www.wawel.com.pl>; open 10am–7pm) is a good place to see the full range.

What to Drink

Though refreshing, Polish beer isn't up to the high standards of brews produced by neighbours Germany, the Czech Republic and Lithuania. Among the best-known brands of Polish beer are Żywiec, Okocim, EB, Warka and Tyskie.

Poland does, however, claim to be the motherland of vodka, which whether true or not doesn't stop the Poles from making some of the best vodka in the world. A baffling battalion of brands awaits the vodka virgin, of which the classiest and cleanest are Belvedere and Chopin (who never touched a drop in his life). Among the many flavoured vodkas the best is Żubrówka, spiced up with a single blade of prairie grass and with a smell and taste like that of a putting green after rain.

Less celebrated is *starka*, a dark and almost syrupy vodka made from rye grain and flavoured with lime flowers and apple leaves. Around since at least the 15th century, *starka* is aged in oak barrels and was traditionally buried in the ground for up to 50 years. This potent spirit can have an alcohol content of over

Café Culture

Kraków's café culture is, like the people who inhabit the city, a rich and varied affair. When the sun is shining, there's perhaps nothing quite as relaxing as sitting under a café umbrella and sipping on a drink accompanied by the sights and sounds of the city. There's even something special about sitting inside a café and watching the rain fall relentlessly for hours on end as it does from time to time. The following cafés represent a mere handful of the city's multitude of outstanding establishments.

In the market square, **Bambus** (Rynek Główny 27) serves good coffee, nibbles and beer in a pleasant atmosphere and is both an excellent spot for a daytime pick-me-up as well as a quiet evening beer. Free wireless internet access provides gives an opportunity to send a few emails home over an espresso.

Huśtawka (ul. św. Tomasza 9) throws together a fine mix of jumble-sale furniture, cold bottled beer and decent hot chocolate. Just around the corner from the Wyspiański Museum *(see page 38)*, expect the place to be overflowing with swotty-looking students.

Miss the **Noworolski** (Rynek Główny 1), in the Cloth Hall, at your peril. This legendary place stands head and shoulders above the rest, with its plush Art Nouveau interior of gorgeous red-and-green velvet rooms and its lovely leather sofas outside. It has a wonderful view of St Mary's Basilica too, and serves excellent cakes and coffee. This was Vladimir Lenin's favourite haunt during his stay in the city between 1912 and 1914.

Two to watch out for in the city centre are Poland's Starbucks wannabes. **Coffeeheaven** (ul. Karmelicka 8) serves the best coffee in town, as well as a good range of sandwiches, wraps and cakes, and is perhaps one of the few places in Poland where smoking is not allowed. The erudite **Massolit Books & Café** (ul. Felicjanek 4) is a cute coffee shop of the carrot-cake variety. Also a strictly non-smoking establishment, it is located inside a bookshop selling by far the best selection of English-language books in the city.

When tipping, one thing to be aware of to avoid an embarrassing and costly situation is that thanking your waiting staff as you hand them your cash is interpreted as an invitation to trouser the change. Save all forms of plaudits until what's owed to you has been safely delivered.

50 percent. Try the excellent Polmos brand from the town of Szczecin, the only word you'll be able to say after a few glasses of the stuff. Slightly less dangerous is the equally unpronounceable Grzaniec Galicyjski, a local herbal wine, which is served heated and flavoured with cloves.

Poland does not produce wine. Imported wines are available, but can be somewhat pricey because of import tax. The cheaper choices are Hungarian and Bulgarian; more expensive are French, Italian and Spanish wines.

Coffee *(kawa)* is a favourite drink and is generally served black (unless you ask for milk) or with a just a dash of milk. Espresso and cappuccino are widely available. Tea *(herbata)*, which is usually served with lemon, is also drunk by most Poles.

To Help You Order...

A table for one/two/ three/four people, please	**Proszę stolik na jedną osobę dwie/trzy/cztery osoby**
Waiter/waitress!	**Proszę pana!/Proszę pani!**
The bill, please.	**Proszę rachunek.**

... and Read the Menu

barszcz	beetroot soup
befsztyk	beef steak
bigos	sauerkraut and meat dish
chleb	bread
frytki	chips/fries
gołąbki	stuffed cabbage leaves
golonka	pork knuckle
grzyb	mushroom
herbata	tea
jarzyny	vegetables
kawa	coffee
kotlet	fried pork cutlet
kurczak	chicken
mięso	meat
ogórek	cucumber
piwo	beer
polędwica	beef
ryba	fish
ser	cheese
szynka	ham
woda	water
wódka	vodka
ziemniaki	potatoes
zrazy	stuffed beef rolls
zupa	soup
żurek	rye-flour soup

Old Town café with a view of St Mary's

HANDY TRAVEL TIPS

An A–Z Summary of Practical Information

A

ACCOMMODATION (see also Camping, Youth Hostels, and the list of Recommended Hotels on page 128)

As Poland's most popular tourist destination, Kraków has ample accommodation of every standard imaginable. From scary hovels run by men in dirty vests to five-star masterpieces complete with receptionists who remember your name, Kraków's got it all. There are hotels, apartments, pensions and hostels to suit every taste, and deciding on where to stay should be based on your needs rather than your budget as prices are well below those of the West. If you are in need of some peace and quiet, you should exercise caution when booking a hotel in the Old Town, which is full of bars and clubs whose existence depends on how much alcohol they can sell, which on a good night translates into noisy streets.

One traditional practice of Polish hotels is to provide free bottles of mineral water. If the bottle's not in the minibar or got a price tag on it, it's yours for free. Breakfast is almost always included in the price of a room, although some hotel breakfasts leave a lot to be desired. Many of the accommodation listings on the Kraków, Tarnów and Zakopane pages at <www.inyourpocket.com> include the option to reserve a room. The website <www.staypoland.com> is also an excellent source for finding and securing exactly the kind of accommodation you're looking for.

I'd like a	**Chciałbym**	*h-tch'ahw*-bim
single/	**pojedynczy/**	po-ye*din*chi/
double room	**podwójny pokój**	po-*dvoo*yni *po*kooy
with a bath	**z wanną**	s *van*-nom
with a shower	**z prysznicem**	s prish*n'ee*-tsem
How much is it	**Ile kosztuje**	*ee*leh kosh*too*yeh
per night?	**noc?**	nots

AIRPORT (see also GETTING THERE)

Kraków's **John Paul II International** (Balice) Airport (ul. Kapitana Medweckiego 1; tel: 012 639 30 00; <www.lotnisko-balice.pl>), 18km (11 miles) east of the city, is small, modern and user-friendly. After passing through passport control and customs, you'll find a small combined arrivals and departures hall on the ground floor, where ATMs and a currency-exchange kiosk (open Mon–Sat 7.45am–8.30pm, Sun 7.45am–7pm) are located, plus a few kiosks where you can buy a Polish SIM card to put in your mobile phone *(see page 123)*.

Getting to the city. The best options are by taxi or train. Ignore the taxi touts and head outside where you'll find plenty of official PT taxis (tel: 91 91) waiting. Make sure the meter is running and expect to pay between 30zł and 50zł. Alternatively, outside the main airport doors is a free bus that takes you to a railway platform where a train runs direct to the city's central train station. Journey time is just 14 minutes, and tickets cost either 4zł or 8zł depending on where you buy your ticket. The service runs regularly every day from around 4am until 11pm. An information desk inside the main terminal building will help you with any other enquiries.

Is there a bus into town?	**Czy jest autobus do centrum?**	chi yest ahw*to*boos do *tsen*trroom
car hire	**wynajmowanie samochodów**	vinuymo-*van*'ye samo-*ho*doof
taxis	**taksówki**	tak*soof*kee

B

BICYCLE HIRE

The mass of bumbling tourists clogging up the Old Town and the combination of trams and idiot drivers in the city centre makes riding a bicycle anywhere but in a park an activity limited to the foolhardy. This doesn't mean renting a bike is impossible, however. Several companies offer bicycles for hire, of which the Kazimierz-based company Two Wheels (ul. Józefa 5; tel: 012 421 57 85; <www.dwakola.neostrada.pl>; open daily 9am–8pm) is arguably the best, hiring bikes for around 30zł a day. Take your passport or driver's licence, leave a 200zł deposit and away you go.

BUDGETING FOR YOUR TRIP

Getting to and sleeping in Kraków are generally the two biggest expenses of a trip to the city. Once these are paid for you'll find that even by Polish standards Kraków is a relatively cheap destination. To work out the mysteries of the Polish *złoty*, see MONEY.

Travel to Kraków. Flying to Kraków has never been cheaper. Return flights from the UK with SkyEurope (Manchester, <www.skyeurope.com>) or Ryanair (London Stansted, <www.ryanair.com>) start from £25. At the top end of the scale, late bookings from Heathrow with the Polish national carrier LOT <www.lot.pl> can cost as much as £400. The only direct flight from the US is with LOT, which flies eight times a week from Chicago. Kraków is a 40-minute hop from Warsaw, so it's also worth looking into flying to Kraków via the capital as this route can turn up the occasional bargain.

Taxis. At the time of writing licensed taxis cost 5zł flagfall plus around 2zł per kilometre after that.

Car hire. Prices range from around 50zł to 200zł per day, and usually include unlimited mileage.

Meals and entertainment. Eating out in Kraków runs from the ridiculously cheap to blowing a week's salary in an upmarket restaurant. Local beer starts at around 6zł for half a litre; beer bought at hotel bars and Guinness in general is more expensive, in some cases costing as much as you would pay in the West. Cinema and theatre tickets remain very affordable, costing somewhere in the region of 10–20zł for a ticket.

Museums and attractions. Almost all museums in the city open their doors once a week for free. The *Kraków In Your Pocket* magazine lists most and includes information on which days are free to visit. Paying to get into a museum is hardly going to ruin you, though. Tickets cost around 5zł, although a full ticket for all the sights at Wawel currently retails at 57zł. Likewise, swimming, ice-skating and even paintballing are relatively cheap.

C

CAMPING

There are several campsites around Kraków, of which the one below is recommended, for both its closeness to the city centre and the fact that it's open year-round. For the multitude of camping opportunities in Zakopane check the official website at <www.zakopane.pl> or drop into the tourist information centre *(see page 125)* when you arrive. Camping is very cheap, with pitches costing from as little as 10zł per night.

Kraków. Smok, ul. Kamedulska 18; tel: 012 429 72 66; <www.camping.krakow.pl>. Just 4km (2½ miles) from the city centre, with excellent facilities and the added attraction of being open all year.

Tarnów. Camping 202, ul. Piłsudskiego 28a; tel: 014 621 51 24; <www.camping.tarnow.pl>. This small and secluded campsite offers excellent-value wooden cabins and tent pitches close to the town centre, plus all the necessary facilities, including a shared kitchen. It's a good budget option if you're touring the region east of Kraków. Open April–November.

CAR HIRE (see also DRIVING)

Kraków's compact size makes hiring a car more trouble than it's worth. However, for visiting other destinations, hiring a car can be a smart move. Bear in mind that the Polish road network leaves much to be desired; roads are in need of repair, and few motorways exist.

Arrangements and conditions for car hire are similar to those in other countries. The minimum age requirement is 21, and you must have been in possession of a valid licence for at least one year. US and Canadian licences are accepted, as are international driving licences. Ask if collision damage waiver insurance is included in the price.

The following companies all have websites in English, and both Europcar and Hertz have offices and cars at the airport:

Avis ul. Lubicz 23; tel: 012 629 61 08; <www.avis.pl>.

Cracowrent ul. Kamieńskiego 41; tel: 012 265 26 50; <www.cracowrent.pl>.

Europcar ul. Szlak 2; tel: 012 633 77 73; <www.europcar.com.pl>.

Hertz al. Focha 1 (inside the Cracovia Hotel); tel: 012 429 62 62; <www.hertz.co.pl>.

Joka ul. Starowiślna 13; tel: 0601 54 53 68; <www.joka.com.pl>.

National ul. Głowackiego 22 (inside the Demel hotel); tel: 012 636 86 30; <www.nationalcar.com.pl>.

Rentacar ul. Piłsudskiego 19; tel: 012 618 43 30; <www.e-rentacar.pl>

Sixt ul. Kapitana Medweckiego 1 (airport); tel: 012 639 32 16; <www.sixt.pl>.

I'd like to hire a car.	**Chcę wynająć samochód**	h-tseh vi*na*yontch' sa*mo*hoot
I'd like it for a day/ a week	**Chcę go na dzień/ tydzień**	h-tseh go na djyeng'/ *ti*djyeng'
What's the charge per day/week?	**Ile to kosztuje za dzień/tydzień?**	*ee*leh to kosh*too*yeh za djyeng'/*ti*djyeng'

CLIMATE

Kraków is somewhat warmer than most Polish cities, although its temperate climate guarantees little more than warmish summers with random lashings of rain. The city generally gets a week or two of blisteringly hot sunshine, but it's impossible to predict when this will happen beyond saying that it might happen in July, which also happens to be the wettest month. Spring and autumn are long, and punctuated by endless overcast days. Winter isn't as predictable as it once was. The long, snowy affairs of the past are becoming less common.

	J	F	M	A	M	J	J	A	S	O	N	D
Min °C	-5	-5	-1	3	9	12	15	14	10	5	1	-2
Max °C	0	1	7	13	20	22	24	23	19	14	6	3
Min °F	23	23	30	37	48	54	59	57	50	41	34	28
Max °F	32	34	45	55	68	72	75	73	66	57	43	37

CLOTHING

Clothes should be packed according to the season, remembering that Polish clouds are fickle. As well as protection against the rain, bring comfortable footwear for use on Kraków's cobblestones. Perhaps the biggest annoyance can be the temperature swings that take place after the sun sets during all but the hottest of summer days. Be prepared, and carry a light jacket or sweater.

There are one or two cultural differences worth noting that might affect what you choose to wear on certain occasions. The Poles like to dress up whenever they can. This means that turning up for the theatre, opera or at a fancy restaurant in anything but a suit or evening dress can lead to embarrassing situations. Although you won't be disowned for looking homeless, you might like to show a little respect. If in doubt, ask first. Likewise, when entering a Catholic church it's considered respectful for men to take off their hats and to keep their legs and, if possible, arms covered. Accordingly, women are advised to cover their shoulders if they don't want to upset the older generation. Men should cover their heads when entering a synagogue. *Yarmulkes* are usually provided when visiting.

CONSULATES AND EMBASSIES

Consulates

UK ul. św. Anny 9; tel: 012 311 00 00; <www.britishembassy.pl>.
US ul. Stolarska 9; tel: 012 424 51 00; <http://poland.usembassy.gov>.

Embassies (in Warsaw)

Australia ul. Nowogrodzka 11; tel: 022 521 34 44; <www.australia.pl>.
Canada ul. Matejki 1/5; tel: 022 584 31 00; <www.canada.pl>.
Republic of Ireland ul. Mysia 5; tel: 022 849 66 33; <www.irlandia.pl>.
South Africa ul. Koszykowa 54; tel: 022 625 62 28; <www.southafrica.pl>.

CRIME AND SAFETY (see also POLICE)

Kraków poses no real threats beyond the occasional petty thief. Don't leave coats hanging around with valuables in the pockets, or leave your mobile phone on a table. Care should also be taken when travelling on busy trams and in any crowded space, especially outdoor concerts. As in any city of this size, exercise caution when walking around late at night. Stick to well-lit streets and if in doubt, use a taxi.

I want to report a theft.	**Chcę zgłosić kradzież.**	h-tseh *z-gwo*sh'eetch' *krra*djyesh
Call the police!	**Wezwijcie policję!**	vez-*veey*-tch'yeh po*leets*-yeh
Help!	**Na pomoc!**	na *po*mots

CUSTOMS AND ENTRY REQUIREMENTS

Holders of EU passports and citizens of Australia, Canada, New Zealand and the United States can enter Poland and stay for up to three months (six months in the case of UK citizens) in any year without a visa. Visas and visa extensions can be applied for from the *Urzad Wojewódzki* (ul. Długa 5). If you're leaving Poland and heading to another EU country you can take up to 10 litres of spirits, 90 litres of wine, 110 litres of beer and 200 cigarettes with you, though there have been stories of these amounts not being accepted in the country of arrival.

D

DISABLED TRAVELLERS

All new buildings and building renovation work in Poland must meet rigid EU standards concerning the provision of facilities for the disabled. Places in Kraków such as the airport, many hotels and quite a few restaurants are now up to Western standards. However, the cobbled streets of the Old Town and most of the best sights within it remain hard work for wheelchair users and travellers with other disabilities. The same also applies for Wawel, Kazimierz and every other destination in this guidebook. Wheelchair users can get around the city fairly easily on public transport. All new 'bendy' buses are designed for wheelchairs, as are trams No. 8, 34, 36 and 38.

DRIVING (see also CAR HIRE)

It's a sobering fact that Polish traffic fatality figures are among the worst in Europe, a testament to the appalling condition of the roads and the often unsafe driving practices of the locals. Poles drive on the right-hand side of the road unless overtaking, which is often done on narrow roads, around bends, and when approaching the brow of a hill.

For those who insist on driving in Kraków, be warned that roadworks are everywhere. If you find yourself following a tram in

Kraków on a stretch of road that doesn't have a separate, fenced-off area for them, proceed with caution. You are expected to stop when trams do, regardless of what lane you're in, as people will be getting on and off, and will be doing so via the road you are driving down.

Note that the stretch of the A4 between Katowice and Kraków is a toll road. Car drivers must pay 6.50zł to use it.

Rules and regulations. You can drive in Poland on an EU licence, although older licences must be accompanied by an International Driving Permit. Dipped headlights must be switched on at all times year round; seat belts are compulsory front and back and the maximum blood-alcohol limit is 0.02 percent.

Petrol. Stations are common on major roads; most stay open around the clock and all sell the full range of petrol, diesel and LPG. At the time of writing, a litre of E98 costs just under 4zł, with LPG slightly less at around 3.50zł.

Speed limits. 130km/h (80mph) on motorways, 110km/h (69mph) on dual carriageways, 100km/h (60mph) on single carriageways, 90km/h (55mph) outside of urban areas, and 50km/h (30mph) in built-up areas. You may be fined on the spot for speeding.

car	**auto/samochód**
petrol station	**stacja benzynowa**
petrol/gas	**benzyna**
unleaded fuel	**benzyna bezołowiowa**
parking	**parking**
detour	**objazd**
stop	**stop**
one-way street	**ulica jednokierunkowa**
no passing	**nie wyprzedzać**

E

ELECTRICITY

All electricity in Poland is 220v AC, 50 Hz. Sockets are the standard round, two-pin European variety with a protruding earth pin. Travellers from the UK, US and others outside continental Europe need to bring an adaptor and/or transformer.

EMERGENCIES (see also POLICE)

The telephone numbers of the three main emergency services are listed below. Unfortunately, your chances of getting an English-speaker at the other end are slim.

Ambulance: **999** Fire: **998** Police: **997**

I want to report an accident.	**Chcę zgłosić wypadek**	h-tseh *z-gwo*sh'eetch' vi*pa*dek
Call a doctor!	**Wezwijcie lekarza!**	vez-*veey*-tch'yeh le*ka*zha
Fire!	**Pali się!**	*pa*lee sh'yeh

G

GAY AND LESBIAN TRAVELLERS

Catholic Poland is a largely conservative country when it comes to social mores, with a far from enlightened attitude to members of its gay community. The age of consent for gays, as well as heterosexuals, is 15.

An excellent gay hotel is listed on *pages 130–1*. Kitsch is the most famous of the city's gay clubs *(see page 86)*. A handy gay guide to the city can be found by following the Kraków links at <www.inyourpocket.com>.

GETTING THERE (see also AIRPORT)

Low-cost flights have wiped out the need for a long bus ride to Kraków. Trains remain popular, but are expensive *(see below)*.

By air. Serving over 2 million passengers a year, Kraków's John Paul II International Airport is the second-busiest airport in Poland after Warsaw. It is served by direct flights to and from Amsterdam, Athens, Barcelona, Birmingham, Bologna, Bonn, Bristol, Brussels, Budapest, Chicago, Cologne, Copenhagan, Cork, Dortmund, Dublin, Frankfurt, Gdańsk, Glasgow, Leeds, Liverpool, London Gatwick, London Luton, London Stansted, Manchester, Milan, Munich, Newcastle, Oslo, Paris, Prague, Rome, Shannon, Stockholm, Stuttgart, Tel Aviv, Vienna and Warsaw. Flight time from London is just over two hours.

Airlines flying in and out of the city include AerLingus, Air France, Alitalia, Austrian Airlines, British Airways, Centralwings, CSA, Direct Fly, easyJet, El Al, Eurolot, Finnair, Germanwings, Jet2.com, LOT, Lufthansa, Malev, Norwegian, Ryanair, SkyEurope, Sterling.dk and Swiss Air.

By rail. International trains arrive in Kraków from Berlin, Bucharest, Budapest, Kiev, Prague and Vienna. It's possible to get to Kraków from London in 23 hours with changes at Brussels and Berlin, where an overnight sleeper leaves every evening and arrives in Kraków the following morning. Kraków's main railway station (Dworzec Główny) is five minutes northeast of the Old Town. ATMs are in the main building if you need cash. All trains to Tarnów and Zakopane leave from this station.

GUIDES AND TOURS

Almost every hotel in Kraków offers at least one tour. Knowing where to go and who to go with can be confusing. The tourist information centres listed on *page 125* give advice on tours, and all have stacks of brochures offering a wide range of trips, ranging from Jewish walking tours of Kazimierz to outings to Wieliczka and Auschwitz. A local company, Tatra Tours & Travel (ul. św. Krzyża 19/1; tel: 012 423 05 27; <www.tatratravel.pl>; open Mon–Sat 9am–5pm), has been in the business longer than most and offers the usual Kraków-based tours as well as hiking and snowmobile adventures in the Tatras. The following three tours are all worth further investigation.

- **Communist.** Take a guided tour of Nowa Huta in an old Trabant with Crazy Guides <www.crazyguides.com>.
- **Papal.** Ride the yellow multimedia Papal Train to Pope John Paul II's birthplace in nearby Wadowice <www.pociag-papieski.pl> .
- **Trams.** Explore the city centre on a vintage tram <www.tramtour.orbis.krakow.pl>.

Is there an English-speaking guide?	**Czy mamy mówiacego po angielsku przewodnika?**	chi *ma*mi moov-yon-*tse*go po an-*g-yel*skoo pshevod-*n'ee*ka

H

HEALTH AND MEDICAL CARE

Visiting Poland poses no great health risks, although precaution is always advisable. UK and EU citizens with a valid European Health Insurance Card (EHIC; available from post offices or online at <www.ehic.org.uk> in the UK) can receive reduced-cost or even free treatment, although private medical insurance is still recommended. Whereas the difference between private and public healthcare in the West is generally a question of waiting time, state healthcare in Poland is of a much lower standard than its private cousin. An English-speaking medical emergency and ambulance telephone service (tel: 012 424 42 00) is available 24 hours a day.

- **24-hour chemist.** Apteka, ul. Galla 26, tel: 012 636 73 65.

Where's the nearest pharmacy?	**Gdzie jest najbliższa apteka?**	g-djyeh yest nay-*bleesh*-sha ap*te*ka

HOLIDAYS

1 January	New Year's Day
March/April	Easter (variable)
1 May	Labour Day
3 May	Constitution Day
June	Corpus Christi (variable)
15 August	Assumption Day
1 November	All Saints' Day
11 November	National Independence Day
25–6 December	Christmas

I

INTERNET CAFÉS

Wireless internet access is widely available without charge in many bars, cafés and shopping centres throughout the city. Internet cafés are now also the favoured place for making cheap or even free Voip telephone calls. The two listed below are both open around the clock:

- **Hetmanska** ul. Bracka 4; tel: 012 429 11 06. A good Internet café offering Skype at no extra cost on every machine.
- **Koffeina** Rynek Główny 23; tel: 012 432 94 94. A proper Internet café that sells decent coffee.

L

LANGUAGE

Polish, along with Czech, Slovakian and Serbian, is one of the western Slavic languages, and is written using Latin letters with the occasional diacritic thrown in to confuse non-speakers. The Poles excel in running consonants together in such a way as to terrify all but the hardiest of polyglots. The good news is that the majority of people working in the tourist industry in Kraków speak good English and/or German. Attempting a few basic words is always a nice thing to do and is appreciated by the locals. As a general rule, the accent falls on the penultimate syllable.

yes	**tak**	tak
no	**nie**	n'yeh
please	**proszę**	*prro*sheh
thank you	**dziękuję**	djyen'*koo*yeh
hi	**cześć**	chesh'tch'
good morning	**dzień dobry**	djyen' *do*brri
good afternoon	**dzień dobry**	djyen' *do*brri
good evening	**dobry wieczór**	dobrri v-yechoorr
good-bye	**do widzenia**	do vee-dzen'ya
Excuse me!/Sorry!	**Przepraszam!**	pshe-*prra*sham
Do you speak English?	**Czy mówi pan po angielsku?**	chi *moo*vee pan po an-*g-yel*skoo
I understand.	**Rozumiem.**	rro-*zoo*m-yem
I don't understand.	**Nie rozumiem.**	n'yeh rro-*zoo*m-yem
My name is...	**Nazywam się**	na*zi*vam sh'yeh
When?	**Kiedy?**	*kye*di
Where is it?	**Gdzie jest?**	g-djyeh yest
on the left	**na lewo**	na *le*vo
on the right	**na prawo**	na *prra*vo
open	**otwarty**	ot-*farr*ti
closed	**zamknięty**	zam-k-*n'yen*ti
old/new	**stary/nowy**	*star*ri/ *no*vi
and/or	**i/albo**	ee/*al*bo
also/but	**również/ale**	*rroov*-n'yesh/*a*-leh

M

MAPS

Free maps can be picked up in tourist information centres, hotels, bars, restaurants and cafés. A good map of Kraków worth buying is Compass' 1:20,000 scale KRAKÓW (6zł), which covers the city in detail, lists public transport routes and has the only decent map of Nowa Huta in print. You can find it in the Empik bookshop listed below.

MEDIA

International newspapers and magazines can be found in better hotels. The Empik bookshop (Rynek Główny 5; tel: 012 429 67 23; open daily 9am–10pm) also stocks a small selection of foreign press, as well as maps. The events website <www.biurofestiwalowe.pl> is complemented by a fine monthly magazine, *Karnet*, available in kiosks and hotels for 4zł. By far the most comprehensive Kraków publication is *Kraków In Your Pocket.* Available for free in magazine format six times a year, the guide is also available without charge in a condensed map format as well as online <www.inyourpocket.com> and in downloadable PDF format. Many of the better hotels in the city come with BBC World and CNN as standard. A couple of sports bars that show Premiership football etc. are listed on *pages 85–6.*

MONEY

The Polish *złoty* (zł) is made up of 100 *groszy*. At the time of writing, 1zł was worth about £0.17, or to put it another way there are about 6zł to £1. ATMs can be found all over Kraków and are the most convenient and economical way of obtaining Polish cash. Currency exchanges *(kantor)* are abundant. Cash still rules in many places, although credit cards are being accepted more and more. Most places in Nowa Huta, Tarnów and Zakopane still only accept cash. Carry some around with you at all times. Traveller's cheques are accepted in most banks, all major hotels and most tourist-oriented shops.

I want to change some dollars/pounds	**Chciałbym wymienić dolary/funty**	*h-tch'ahw*-bim vi*m-yen*itch' do*la*rri/*foon*ti
What's the exchange rate?	**Jaki jest kurs waluty?**	*ya*kee yest koors va*loo*ti

OPENING TIMES

Banks. Banks open early, usually at 8am and stay open until around 6pm. Most banks are closed during the weekend.

Shops. Most shops open at either 9am or 10am, stay open until about 6pm, work shorter hours on Saturdays and are normally closed on Sundays. Exceptions include shops inside big shopping malls *(see page 88)*, and markets, of which the latter are open by 5am and generally stay open until the middle of the afternoon.

Bars and restaurants. Cafés selling alcohol open at about 8am, while bars opening any time between 10am and 10pm and stay open well into the night. For restaurant opening times *see page 134*.

Museums and galleries. These generally open at 10am, and close at any time from 2pm to 6pm. Most museums don't open on a Monday.

Monday	**poniedziałek**	pon'ye-*djyah*wek
Tuesday	**wtorek**	*fto*rrek
Wednesday	**środa**	*sh'rro*da
Thursday	**czwartek**	*ch-farr*tek
Friday	**piątek**	*p-yon*tek
Saturday	**sobota**	so*bo*ta
Sunday	**niedziela**	n'ye*djye*la
tomorrow	**jutro**	*yoo*trro

P

POLICE (see also CRIME AND SAFETY and EMERGENCIES)

You'll often spot police on the beat in the Old Town, where there's a police station *(posterunek policji)* at Rynek Główny 27. An English- and German-speaking police hotline (tel: 0800 20 03 00 from a landline, tel: +48 22 601 55 55 if roaming) has recently been set up, which is currently only staffed from 10am to 10pm.

Where's the nearest police station?	**Gdzie jest najbliższy komisariat?**	g-djyeh yest nuy-*bleesh*-shi komee*sarr*-yat
My ... has been stolen	**Ukradli mi ... z mojego samochadu**	oo*krrad*-lee mee ... z mo*y*ego samo-*ho*doo
wallet	**portfel**	*porrt*-fel
handbag	**torebkę**	to*rrep*-keh
passport	**paszport**	*pash*porrt

POST OFFICES

Kraków's main post office (Poczta Główna) is just east of the Old Town on the corner of ul. Wielopole at ul. Westerplatte 20 (tel: 012 422 66 96; open Mon–Fri 7.30am–8.30pm, Sat 8am–2pm, Sun 9am–2pm). A baffling queue ticket system is in operation, although stamps can be bought without queuing at windows 2–14. Stamps for postcards and letters abroad cost 2.40zł, or 1.30zł if you're

A stamp for this postcard/ letter please	**Proszę znaczek na tę pocztówkę/ list**	*prro*sheh *z-na*check na teh poch-*toof*keh/ leest
airmail	**lotniczą**	lot*n'ee*chom
registered	**pocztą poleconą**	*poch*tom pole*tso*-nom

sending them within Poland. There's a small post office inside Wawel's main ticket office (open daily 9am–4pm), which is never busy and has English-speaking staff. Postboxes are scattered around the city and are red with a yellow post horn set against a blue background. Once you've deposited your mail in one, don't hold your breath. It's not uncommon for letters to take at least a week to reach the UK.

PUBLIC TRANSPORT

Public transport in Kraków is both cheap and reliable. The fabulous tram system provides the perfect way of getting around, from 5am to 11pm. Tram tickets cost 2.50zł per ride on one tram over any distance. Better value are 24-hour, 48-hour and 72-hour tickets, costing 10.40zł, 18.80zł and 25zł respectively. Buy them from most kiosks or anywhere you see a 'Sprzedaż Biletów MPK' sign. Tickets must be validated in one of the yellow machines on boarding. People travelling on a single 2.50zł ticket who are in possession of items bigger than 20 x 40 x 60cm (8 x 16 x 24in) need to buy a ticket for that as well. Be careful when getting off trams in the city centre, where they share the roads with cars. You're essentially stepping down into traffic.

I'd like a ... ticket to ... please.	**Proszę bilet ... do ...**	*prro*sheh *bee*let do
single (one-way)	**w jedną stronę**	v *yed*-nom *strro*neh
return (round trip)	**powrotny**	povrrotni

Taxis. If you want to stay the right side of bankrupt, the golden rule is: when you want a taxi, always choose licensed ones. These are easily recognisable by a large light on the roof displaying the company's name and telephone number.

Barbakan, tel: 96 61 **Euro**, tel: 96 64 MPT, tel: 91 91

R

RELIGION

The Poles have been proud Catholics for over a thousand years, a fact borne out by the Vatican's decision in 1978 to elect the first non-Italian pontiff in over 400 years. Pope John Paul II rose through the ranks in Kraków and returned to the city more than once. He's considered by the nation as one of the main driving forces behind the collapse of Communism. His image can be found everywhere, and he remains an enormous focus of pride for the country.

T

TELEPHONES

Public telephones. The combined internet and mobile phone revolution has all but seen the death of public telephones in Poland. If you can actually find one, a Kraków public telephone is either yellow or silver and works using prepaid cards bought from any shop selling sweets and cigarettes. To find out more about where to make Voip calls in Kraków, see INTERNET CAFÉS.

Mobile phones. Avoid roaming costs by putting a local prepaid SIM card in your mobile phone. Several companies now offer ridiculously cheap start-up packages for less than 10zł, with top-up cards costing 5zł and upwards. Both can be bought from shops and kiosks around the city as well as the airport, bus and railway stations and the Empik bookshop listed under MEDIA.

Making the call. To call Kraków from outside the country, dial your international access code followed by 48 for Poland and the subscriber number minus the initial 0. The 012 at the start of a Kraków number is both part of the number and the code for the city. If you're calling Kraków from anywhere in Poland on a landline you simply

dial the 10-digit number. The same applies for calling a landline from a Polish mobile with the exception of Plus GSM, which requires the dropping of the first 0. To get a line out of Poland, dial 00 plus whatever you need after that for the country in question.
National Operator tel: 912 **International Operator** tel: 901

telephone card	**karta telefoniczna**	*karr*teh tele-fon*eech*-nom

TIME DIFFERENCES

Poland is on Central European Time (CET), which is one hour ahead of GMT. As in the rest of Europe, the clocks go forward one hour on the last Sunday of March and back again on the last Sunday of October.

New York	London	**Kraków**	Jo'burg	Sydney	Auckland
6am	11am	**noon**	noon	8pm	10pm

TIPPING

A typical restaurant or bar employee in Kraków earns an average 750zł (£125) every month. Needless to say, tipping is more than welcome. As Poland becomes increasingly Westernised, tipping is slowly taking over from what went before it, namely a gracious compliment on the quality of the service performed and no more. Tipping is now firmly established in the Old Town and much of Kazimierz, the usual sum being 10 percent or a rounding up of the bill, but it's still a rare occurrence in the suburbs as well as in Tarnów and Zakopane. *(See also box on page 102).*

TOILETS

The quintessential Polish toilet is a rather unsavoury affair guarded by a grumpy old lady whose job is to collect money (anything up to 2zł) and hand out a standard two squares of toilet paper. The sight is slowly vanishing but is still surprisingly common, even in such places as Wawel, where the toilets have been renovated but the old lady remains. The Poles like to keep you guessing when you're desperate, putting a triangle on the door for men and a circle for women. Public toilets simply don't exist, and trying to use one in a restaurant or café where you're not a customer can be difficult to say the least. McDonald's even goes so far as to employ somebody to check you're in possession of a valid receipt before using their facilities. The shopping malls listed on *page 89* have free toilet facilities.

men's toilet	**męski (panowie)**
women's toilet	**damski (panie)**

TOURIST INFORMATION

Old Town pl. Mariacki 3; tel: 012 431 16 78. Open Mon–Sat 9am–7pm, Sun 9am–3pm.
Kazimierz ul. Józefa 7; tel: 012 432 01 10. Open Mon–Fri 10am–6pm.
Nowa Huta os. Słoneczne 16; tel: 012 643 03 03. Open Tues–Sat 10am–2pm.
Tarnów Rynek 7; tel: 014 688 90 90; <www.it.tarnow.pl>. Open Mon–Fri 8am–8pm, Sat–Sun 9am–5pm.
Zakopane ul. Kościuszki 17; tel: 018 201 22 11; <www.zakopane.pl>. Open daily 9am–6pm.

Małopolska Tourist Information Rynek Główny 1/3; tel: 012 421 77 06. Located inside the eastern side of the Cloth Hall, this great little tourist information centre is the best place in town to come if you're looking to explore anywhere outside of the city. Essential visiting for anyone wanting to get the most out of a trip to Tarnów or Zakopane. Open Mon–Fri 9am–6pm, Sat–Sun 9am–2pm.

For general information before you leave home, write to or call the Polish National Tourism Office or visit its website:

UK: Polish National Tourist Office, Level 3, Westgate House, West Gate, London W5 1YY; tel: 08700 675012; fax: 08700 675011; <www.visitpoland.org>.

US: Polish National Tourist Office, 5 Marine View Plaza, Hoboken, NJ 07030; tel: 201 420 9910; fax: 201 584 9153; <www.polandtour.org>.

W

WEBSITES

The official Kraków tourist information website is at <www.krakow.pl>. *Kraków In Your Pocket* offers free information on everything in the city from tourist sights and hotels to laundries and nightclubs. Read more at <www.inyourpocket.com>. The excellent <www.cracowonline.com> lists most events in the city, ranging from exhibitions to Dada theatre.

Kraków boasts more churches than any general guidebook such as this could ever cover. A very good site for those interested in churches is <www.krakow-info.com>, which also has more general information about the city.

YOUTH HOSTELS

With more than 60 hostels in the city, ranging from far-flung fleapits to city-centre party hostels, making the right decision about where to stay can be daunting. With the exception of the legendary Nathan's, all of the following hostels are suitable for every kind of budget traveller regardless of age or lifestyle preference. Keep in mind that hotel prices in Kraków are much lower than in most Western countries, so hostels are only really worth considering if you're on the very tightest of budgets.

Good Bye Lenin ul. Joselewicza 23; tel: 012 421 20 30; <www.goodbyelenin.pl>. Pandering to the next generation of *Ostalgie* aficionados, the Good Bye Lenin hostel offers a rather limp Communist experience that fails to go beyond the surface of the assorted commie propaganda posters scattered about the walls. But it's a good and central hostel all the same. Most major credit cards accepted.

Hostel Rynek 7 Rynek Główny 7/6; tel: 012 431 16 98; <www.hostelrynek7.com>. The dormitories here look out onto the Rynek and Cloth Hall; the twin rooms are at the back of the building. This is a pleasant and relaxed place, with good security and the opportunity to fall into bed from any one of hundreds of bars and clubs within easy walking distance.

Mama's ul. Bracka 4; tel: 012 429 59 40; <www.mamashostel.com.pl>. Possibly the most feminine hostel in Kraków, Mama's provides a good base at a good price and little else. It's more peaceful than many, and the Old Town location is one of the best there is. Most major credit cards accepted.

Nathan's Villa ul. św. Agnieszki 1; tel: 012 422 35 45; <www.nathansvilla.com>. On offer here are a battalion of bunk beds and a handful of more intimate rooms in the city's notorious and decidedly raucous party hostel. The cellar bar can get lively to say the least, but if you're a hard-core hosteller looking for everything that a hostel is supposed to be, you won't find a better choice. Most major credit cards accepted.

Recommended Hotels

The following represents a small selection of some of the more interesting places to stay in Kraków and in Tarnów and Zakopane, the two major excursion destinations included in this guidebook. For a range of apartment-rental options across Kraków, check out NorPol *(see page 129)* and Affinity Flats *(see page 131)*.

Prices indicate a double room including breakfast during the high season, which kicks off around the start of June and finishes towards the end of September. Booking in advance is advisable year-round, and absolutely essential during the high season.

Hotel room rates may be quoted in US dollars, euros and Polish złoty – though the bill will ultimately be rendered in złoty. All establishments listed here accept major credit cards, except where noted.

$$$$	over 500zł
$$$	300–500zł
$$	150–300zł
$	below 150zł

OLD TOWN

Copernicus $$$$ *ul. Kanonicza 16, tel: 012 424 34 00, <www.hotel.com.pl>*. The Copernicus, parts of which date from the 14th century, is located on the city's oldest street *(see page 42)* and features some breathtaking views of Wawel. Facilities include vast Jacuzzis, a fine restaurant and a glorious rooftop terrace during the summer. A favourite with visiting VIPs. If you can afford it, this is money well spent indeed – you'll have a truly memorable stay.

Francuski $$$ *ul. Pijarska 13, tel: 012 627 37 77, <www.orbis.pl>*. This handsome Orbis hotel, built in 1912, is on the edge of the Old Town, facing the Planty near the old city wall. Rooms are luxurious and traditional in style. Wheelchair access.

Grand $$$$ *ul. Sławkowska 5/7, tel: 012 421 72 55, <www.grand.pl>*. Putting people to bed for over a century, the Grand Hotel, with its wonderfully over-the-top decor, has effortless charm and sophistication. It's the perfect place to celebrate life with all the luxury trimmings, and is superbly located a short distance from the Rynek. Extras include a magnificently decorated restaurant and café, plus the kind of service that you get only at prices like this.

NorPol Apartments $$$ *ul. Szczepańska 7, tel: 012 431 14 24, <www.norpol-apartments.com>*. A range of good-looking apartments from matchbox-size to palaces throughout the city centre (note that it's listed here under Old Town because that's where the office is). Although they don't like pets or smokers, they can offer a range of add-ons, including airport pick-up and day trips. Long-term rental is also available.

Pod Różą $$$ *ul. Floriańska 14, tel: 012 424 33 00, <www.hotel.com.pl>*. An awesome hotel that welcomes you with a sharp click of its automatic wooden doors. The casual-looking reception masks the opulence of the rooms upstairs, which are fitted out with fine antiques as well as the latest gadgets. The hotel also has two restaurants and a vinoteka.

Pollera $$$ *ul. Szpitalna 30, tel: 012 422 10 44, <www.pollera.com.pl>*. A fabulous Art Nouveau masterpiece in an equally good location, the historic Pollera offers surprisingly good value with all the trimmings. It also has a fantastic Wyspiański stained-glass window as its focal point. This is the ideal location for anyone visiting with an eye to the finer things the city has to offer.

Saski $$ *ul. Sławkowska 3, tel: 012 421 42 22, <www.hotelsaski.com.pl>*. Located inside a classic 16th-century Old Town building just north of the Rynek, the Saski positively oozes charm and eccentricity. Like a distant aunt whose wealth has dwindled, the hotel strives to hold onto its dignity amid a sea of rococo flourishes and wobbly furniture. Brimming with personality and recommended for this alone.

Stary $$$$ *ul. Szczepańska 5, tel: 012 384 08 08, <www.stary.hotel.com.pl>*. Everything is impeccable here, from a renovation job that perfectly melds old and new elements, to staff who are genuinely pleased to help. To top it all, a rooftop bar with a splendid view of the Rynek provides a wonderful place to unwind during the summer.

Trecius $$ *ul. św. Tomasza 18, tel: 012 421 25 21, <www.trecius.krakow.pl>*. At the time of writing, Trecius offers just six pension-style rooms in the heart of the Old Town, but there are more in the pipeline. Clean, quirky and beautiful, the rooms come with satellite television, great showers and a price tag that would be a bargain at twice the price. Excellent-value accommodation.

Wit Stwosz $$$ *ul. Mikołajska 28, tel: 012 429 60 26, <www.wit-stwosz.com.pl>*. The Wit Stwosz is named after the medieval German master carver whose contributions to the city are many and great. The master clearly didn't have a hand in decorating the rooms here, which are nevertheless tastefully decorated in a style harking back to the glory days of the 19th century. The hotel is very well located in a 16th-century town house just two minutes' walk from the Rynek. As is almost standard throughout the centre of the city, there is a lovely-looking restaurant in a charming brick cellar.

KAZIMIERZ

Tournet $ *ul. Miodowa 7, tel: 012 292 00 88, <www.accommodation.krakow.pl>*. Cheap and cheerful pension accommodation in the heart of Kazimierz, featuring spartan, but comfortable rooms with Ikea-type fittings, showers and a kettle. The more expensive rooms are essentially the same, only with a television, which you're probably not going to watch anyway.

WEST OF THE OLD TOWN

2nd Floor $$ *ul. Nowowiejska, tel: 012 294 56 99, <www.2ndfloor.queer.pl>*. With a room called the Queer Studio and advice given to gay guests on what to do and where to go in Kraków, 2nd Floor should be applauded for its work in what remains a predominantly anti-gay city. This very gay hotel is clean and friendly, with budget furniture and plenty of pink splashes. The Old Town is only 15 minutes' walk away. Breakfast isn't included, but there's a kitchen here if you want to make it yourself.

Affinity Flats $$$ *ul. Karmelicka 7, tel: 012 430 08 18, <www.affinityflats.com>*. Arguably the best apartment-rental people in Kraków, Affinity offers a range of options, from budget boxes away from the centre to plush pads in the Old Town. The slightly steep prices are worth paying because you get good service and a guarantee that what you see is what you get. Check out their website for more information.

Cracovia $$ *al. Focha 1, tel: 012 424 56 00, <www.orbis.pl>*. During the Communist era, the Cracovia played host to visiting Party officials, and little has been done to modernise this giant concrete edifice since then. If you're looking for an authentic blast-from-the-past experience and don't mind the possibility of sharing breakfast with a bus load of German tourists, the Cracovia is for you.

EAST OF THE OLD TOWN

Monopol $$ *ul. św. Gertrudy 6, tel: 012 422 76 66, <www.rthotels.com.pl>*. A one-time Commie staple, the Monopol has been tidied up and now caters mostly to tour groups who favour its combination of pleasant rooms and good facilities, proximity to the Old Town and down-to-earth prices. On a busy tram route and nicely situated between the Old Town and Kazimierz.

Wielopole $$ *ul. Wielopole 3, tel: 012 422 14 75, <www.wielopole.pl>*. Another bargain treat midway between the Old Town and Kazimierz. With a spartan interior, the Wielopole stands out for the polished attitude of the staff, who can never do enough for you. The rooms are basic, with simple showers, cable television and free internet in every room. Breakfast is included in the price.

NOWA HUTA

Santorini $$ *ul. Bulwarowa 35b, tel: 012 680 51 95, <www.santorini.krakow.pl>*. If you've got a car or are really interested in Nowa Huta then the Santorini will be right up your street. Offering very good value, this fairly new hotel features classic mid-range rooms with satellite television, internet access and minibars. The in-house restaurant *(see page 141)* isn't going to win any awards, but it's by far the best place to eat in the area.

TARNÓW

As with Zakopane *(see opposite page)*, a visit to Tarnów can easily be turned into something longer than a day trip. The three options listed here are the tip of the accommodation iceberg. For information about more hotels in the city, see the tourist information website at <www.it.tarnow.pl> or drop into the Tourist Information Centre *(see below)* when you arrive.

Tarnovia $$ *ul. Kościuszki 10, tel: 014 630 03 50, <www.hotel.tarnovia.pl>*. A 1970s-built masterpiece and recommended just for its socialist charm and bizarre decor, the Tarnovia has rooms that come in a wide range of options, from unrenovated shoeboxes to a handful of spruced-up rooms bordering on business class. Close to the railway and bus stations, this could be just the one you're looking for.

Tourist Information Centre $ *Rynek 7, tel: 014 688 90 90, <www.it.tarnow.pl>*. Tarnów's Tourist Information Centre offers its own guest rooms overlooking the main market square. Rooms are clean and comfortable, cheap and convenient. Having a valuable source of local information downstairs is another good reason to choose this place, as are the unexpected additions, including free wireless internet throughout. This is the best accommodation bargain in town. Cash only.

U Jana $$ *Rynek 14, tel: 014 626 05 64, <www.hotelujana.pl>.* An interior that's a peculiar mix of bygone splendour and bling awaits guests of U Jana. The rooms are large, featuring lovely wooden floors, huge double beds and refreshing showers, but the service here leaves something to be desired.

ZAKOPANE

Bearing in mind that Zakopane receives 50 times its population in tourists annually, it's vital to book a hotel if you're planning to stay during the high seasons of summer (June–September) or winter (Christmas–March).

Gospoda Pod Niebem $ *ul. Droga Stanisława Zubka 5, tel: 018 206 29 09, <www.podniebem.zakopane.pl>.* Gospoda Pod Niebem is a charming albeit basic wooden house on top of Gubałówka Hill above Zakopane. Expect little in the way of extras like trouser presses or room service, but do prepare yourself for the invigorating smell of pine, more fresh air than you could ever wish for, and a fantastic view of the Tatras. The rooms come with a bed, television, shower and little else, but for the price and the location you can't really do better.

Grand Hotel Stamary $$$ *ul. Gościuszki 19, tel: 018 202 45 10, <www.stamary.pl>.* A strange location next to the bus station for such a fine hotel as this, but this is Poland after all. The Grand has luxurious rooms with all the trimmings, very well-mannered staff, spa facilities and the best espressos in town – you get what you pay for here, which is a lot. The Grand is highly recommended if your budget allows.

Litwor $$$$ *ul. Krupówki 40, tel: 018-201 71 90, <www.litwor.pl>.* Located on a small square off Zakopane's main shopping promenade, this large, handsome traditional hotel is one of the choicest places to stay in town, and comes with a matching price tag. It has a delightful lobby bar, great restaurant, nicely furnished rooms, an indoor swimming pool and fitness centre with sauna. Wheelchair access.

Recommended Restaurants

In the city where Lenin once sipped tea and brewed a revolution, Kraków offers everything to stave off hunger pains, from sticky buns and *pierogi* to slap-up curries and the full Polish experience. The following price guide refers to a three-course meal for one person, excluding drinks. For a more in-depth look at Polish food and drink, *see page 94.* A list of the city's best cafés can be found on *page 101.* All the restaurants mentioned below accept most major credit cards, unless otherwise noted. Booking in advance is recommended to guarantee a table.

$$$$	over 200zł
$$$	100–200zł
$$	50–100zł
$	below 50zł

OLD TOWN

Not surprisingly, the Old Town features the best choice of restaurants in the city, from kebab stalls selling spicy lamb and falafel delicacies to ostentatious tourist traps with white tablecloths and Western prices. The Old Town is also the best place to try traditional Polish fare in fairytale surroundings.

Aqua e Vino $$$ *ul. Wiślna 5/10, tel: 012 421 25 67.* A great Italian restaurant with attached lounge bar, run by an Italian and thus ensuring you get both authenticity and quality. The minimalist decor includes large black-and-white photographs of famous people eating Italian food, of which the stuff served here is arguably the best in Kraków. There's a fine wine list to accompany the food too. Highly recommended. Open daily noon–midnight.

Babci Maliny $ *ul. Sławkowska 17, tel: 012 422 76 01.* A rather whimsical take on Polish food deep in the bowels of a large library, this classic family favourite serves excellent-value *pierogi* and other traditional Polish dishes in a setting that could easily double as the set for a children's television programme. If you don't mind eating your dinner off a log amid tropical fish and other quirky trappings, you'll simply love this one. Open Mon–Fri 11am–7pm, Sat–Sun noon– 7pm. Cash only.

Cyrano de Bergerac $$$$ *ul. Sławkowska 26, tel: 012 411 72 88.* Ask anyone in the tourist industry where to go for the best meal in Kraków and the chances are they'll mention this place, which represents French dining opulence in the extreme. The menu includes such delights as foie gras, ostrich and something called a Crazy Salad. To give an indication of what you'll be expected to cough up for eating here, bottles of champagne run to 1,250zł. Open Mon–Sat noon–midnight. Closed Sun.

Green Way $$ *ul. Mikołajska 14, tel: 012 431 10 27.* A haven for non-meat-eaters, this restaurant serves excellent vegetarian food with plenty of experimental touches. The dishes here are enormous, delicious and as cheap as buttons. The setting inside a gorgeous Old Town building not far from St Mary's Basilica only adds to the positive experience. Open Mon–Fri 10am–10pm, Sat and Sun 11am–9pm.

Metropolitan $$ *ul. Sławkowska 3, tel: 012 421 98 03.* As you walk in, you're greeted by the delicious odour of frying bacon, confirming the Metropolitan's reputation as the best all-day breakfast venue in the city. Bustling waitresses, wood-panelled walls, chess sets and a fine English menu all add up to set off this place as a major culinary accomplishment. Open Mon–Sat 7am–midnight, Sun 7am–10pm.

Miód Malina $$ *ul. Grodzka 40, tel: 012 430 04 11.* Unaware of the significance of the raspberry to British humour, the proprietor has seen fit to paint a number of large purple ones on the walls here. This, however, doesn't stop the hordes of tourists and tour groups, who regularly pack the place out for the purpose of eating from a fine Italian menu. Open daily noon–11pm.

Młyn $ *ul. Sienna 12, tel: 012 422 23 62.* Cheap Polish canteen nosh in an ambience of hanging foliage. Młyn is both a café and a restaurant, so you can come by for just a coffee or have something more substantial. Its menu is not going to win any culinary awards, but for good-value, filling food and a nice variety of local diners it's a good place to visit all the same. Open Mon–Fri 8am–midnight, Sat–Sun 9am–midnight.

North Fish $$ *Rynek Główny 25, tel: 012 431 19 87.* A standard fish-and-chip restaurant with added extras, such as grilled tuna and salmon plus a salad bar and beer and wine. The fish is generally good, and comes in all the usual battered varieties, including cod fillet in spicy batter. They'll also keep you amused with nice little touches like ketchup served inside ice cream cones. Open daily 11am–10pm.

Padre $$$ *ul. Wiślna 11, tel: 012 422 08 66.* A charming terrace during the summer and a gorgeous and unpretentious cellar restaurant for the colder months, Padre boasts a pair of Italian and Indian chefs who churn out decent dishes from their respective national cuisines. The waitresses are pleasant enough and the piped music is always entertaining. Open Mon–Fri 11am–11pm, Sat–Sun noon–11pm.

Paese $$$ *ul. Poselska 24, tel: 012 421 62 73.* Attempting to recreate a Corsican village feel in Poland is bound to miss the mark, but that's no reason to give this boat-themed restaurant a wide berth. Both the food and the service are outstanding (visiting groups should try one of the marvellous fondues), and its location, cunningly hidden in one of the Old Town's lesser-known back-streets, tends to keep the hordes away. Open daily noon–11pm.

Pod Osłonà Nieba $ *ul. Grodzka 26, tel: 012 423 23 08.* Budget food served from metal containers with the added bonus of a classy bar, this is Poland at its best. Nutritious and filling, the food isn't exactly cordon bleu, but at prices like these you can't expect it. They also do a good takeaway, but make sure you stand in the right queue. The huddle of hungry locals standing by the entrance are waiting for kebabs. Slip by them and you'll cut waiting time in half. Open daily 10am–midnight.

Redolfi $$ *Rynek Główny 38, tel: 012 423 05 79.* Redolfi is an excellent café and lunch spot during the day and a better than average French restaurant during the evening. The refreshingly unpretentious interior of Redolfi is often packed with a pleasant mix of locals and tourists. The menu includes several Provençal dishes as well as the recommended veal roulades, and its ringside seat on the Rynek can't be beaten as a location. Open daily 9am–midnight.

U Zalipianek $ *ul. Szewska 24, tel: 012 422 29 50.* Kraków's undisputed number-one anomaly, this bizarre little restaurant features an old lady who looks after your coats, traditional flowery folk-art murals on the walls, excellent value potato pancakes and, during the summer, a lovely terrace in the Planty. In business since Communist times, it remains a firm favourite among the city's tea-fuelled grannies and is well worth a visit. A classic. Open daily 9am–10pm. Cash only.

Wierzynek $$$$ *Rynek Główny 15, tel: 012 424 96 00.* In business since 1364, Kraków's oldest restaurant features a labyrinth of smart rooms, waitresses in 18th-century costumes, a frighteningly expensive range of regal Polish food including a good selection of game, and an illustrious guest book including such names as De Gaulle and Castro. The latter was brought here under protest as he was in Kraków to observe a revolution, not hobnob with the nomenklatura. Open daily 1pm–midnight.

Zapiecek Polskie Pierogarnie $ *ul. Sławkowska 32, tel: 012 422 74 95.* Delicious *pierogi* the size of pillows are served on plastic plates in this tiny five-table restaurant, which is always packed to the rafters. Good value indeed, the menu is limited to the aforementioned fare and a few salads, plus there's the added bonus of a culinary challenge: if you can eat 59 *pierogi* in less than 25 minutes you can eat for free. A good place to stoke up your engine while taking in the sights of the Old Town. Open daily 10am–9pm. Cash only.

KAZIMIERZ

With the exception of one or two fine restaurants, notably Jewish ones, Kazimierz's reputation is intrinsically linked with its excellent bar and café culture.

Alef $$$ *ul. Szeroka 17, tel: 012 421 38 70.* With a decor of antiques and various Jewish bits and pieces, Alef serves average food that includes such unlikely sounding dishes as *shubaha* herring and beetroot soup with *kreplach*. A good reason for a visit here is the excellent nightly live Jewish and Roma music that adds to the entire experience rather than getting in the way. Not the best Jewish dining food in town, but for ambience and a decent night out for the whole family you can't really beat this one. Open daily 9am–10pm.

Ariel $$$ *ul. Szeroka 18, tel: 012 421 79 20.* The somewhat cluttered decor gives this restaurant the look of a curiosity shop, but if you're in town and looking for a Jewish dining experience it's worth putting Ariel on your list. The food swerves perilously from mediocre to sublime, but the live music is always fun. Open daily 10am–midnight.

Bagelmama $$ *ul. Podbrzezie 2, tel: 012 431 19 42.* Bagelmama serves a beguiling hotchpotch of bagels and Mexican food. The rather chatty owner can spoil the food at times, but there's no getting away from the fact that the bagels served here outshine those on offer in the rest of the country. Open Tues–Thur 10am–9pm, Fri–Sat 10am–10pm. Cash only.

Bombaj Tandoori $$ *ul. Szeroka 7, tel: 012 422 37 97.* The Bombaj possesses Kraków's solitary tandoori oven, but this is not really a guarantee that anyone knows how to use it, as evidenced by mixed reports about the quality of the food dished up here. When it's good it's good, and in all fairness there's no better Indian restaurant in the city, despite the rather lacklustre attempts at decoration. Open Sun–Sat noon–11pm, Fri–Sat noon–midnight.

Brasserie $$ *ul. Gazowa 4, tel: 012 292 19 98.* Located inside a former tram garage, the quirky Brasserie features huge people-watching windows, a nice mix of patrons and a fabulous menu of international dishes including frogs' legs in breadcrumbs, some huge and tasty salads and a wide range of vegetarian options. Its location down an otherwise nondescript street means there are usually a few tables available when the rest of Kazimierz's eating houses are packed to capacity. Open daily noon–11pm.

Edo $$$ *ul. Bożego Ciała 3, tel: 012 422 24 24.* Better than average, good-value Japanese food including great sushi in an equally fine restaurant. Although it's unlikely you're in Poland especially for the Japanese food, bear in mind that the prices make it an extremely attractive option. The private area at the back does the full no-shoes affair. Book early to avoid disappointment. Open Sun–Wed noon–10pm, Thur–Sat noon–11pm.

Klezmer Hois $$$ *ul. Szeroka 6, tel: 012 411 12 45.* Housed inside the district's former Jewish bathhouse, this is fine and traditional Jewish dining at its best. The food and the surroundings make for a perfect night out, and of course there's lively Jewish music to keep the tourists happy. Of the three Jewish restaurants listed here, Klezmer Hois is most certainly the best option. Open daily 10am–10pm.

Momo $ *ul. Józefa Dietla 49, tel: 0603 92 64 79.* Famous throughout Poland, this small and unassuming wholefood and vegetarian restaurant between the Old Town and Kazimierz provides good healthy food, from brown-rice dishes to a range of excellent salads. Don't be put off by the canteen appearance – there are some truly appetising dishes on offer here, representing excellent value. Open daily 11am–8pm. Cash only.

WEST OF THE OLD TOWN

Avanti Orangerie $$ *ul. Karmelicka 7, tel: 012 430 07 10.* Avanti Orangerie has a good Italian menu with a few Tuscan specialities. With its indoor plants and glass roof, dining in this favoured haunt of the city's burgeoning business-lunch set is a bit like eating in a greenhouse. There's a more formal restaurant in the cellar which, like the Orangerie, is highly recommended. One quibble: the service could be a little faster. Open daily noon–10pm.

Rózowy Słoń $ *ul. Straszewskiego 24, tel: 012 422 10 00.* Catering to the local budget student community, the Pink Elephant numbers among one of Kraków's more eccentric restaurants. The decor features pink-and-green furniture, and the walls are plastered with comic-strip murals. This may not be the most comfortable of environments to eat in, but if you can stomach the luminous overload you'll be rewarded with dirt-cheap Polish food and a fairly decent salad bar. Open Mon–Sat 9am–8pm, Sun 11am–7pm. Cash only.

EAST OF THE OLD TOWN

San Sebastian $$ *ul. św. Sebastiana 25, tel: 012 429 24 76.* San Sebastian specialises in fine nouvelle cuisine and also features a monster list of deadly cocktails. Unlike the food, however, the service leaves a lot to be desired. Highly recommended at any time of day or night is their pâté starter. This establishment is proof that the Poles can cook cuisine other than their own to a high standard. Open Mon–Sat 8am–11pm, Sun 9am–11pm.

NOWA HUTA

Following the recent push to attract coachloads of tourists to Nowa Huta, tourist authorities hope that a few decent places to eat will follow in their wake. At the time of writing the district remains sadly lacking in anything really worth sticking around for, and the following have been included more as curiosities rather than anything to write home about.

Cocktail Bar $ *os. Centrum C, tel: 012 644 28 07.* Every working-class district needs its own working-class café-bar, and this is Nowa Huta's. The burgers and sausages on offer are only a little less sickly than the multicoloured walls, which are only slightly less colourful than the colourful characters who frequent the place. Open Mon–Fri 10am–midnight, Sat–Sun 11am–1pm. Cash only.

Santorini $$$ *ul. Bulwarowa 35b, tel: 012 644 91 11.* Inside the hotel of the same name *(see page 132)*, this is Nowa Huta's first foray into the world of white tablecloths and immaculate-looking waiters. It provides an interesting mix of local and international dishes, of which the latter should be avoided. Open daily 10am–10pm.

TARNÓW

As one would expect for a provincial Polish town such as Tarnów, the quality of available dining establishments is somewhat limited. Still, it's hungry work tramping the streets, and if you choose to spend the night here you'll almost certainly need to eat something.

Ke Maro $$ *ul. Żydowska 13, tel: 014 627 64 45.* Worth the trip to Tarnów alone, this extraordinary Roma restaurant features three rooms decorated according to different aspects of Roma life, boasts a spectacular menu of Roma dishes, and is run by a gregarious Roma family who like nothing more than to make visitors welcome (don't be surprised if the entire clan come in for a look at you while you're eating). There's often live music too, making popping in for a quick bite to eat something that can turn into a prolonged and exceedingly enjoyable affair. Highly recommended. Open daily 11am–2am. Cash only.

Tarnovia $$ *ul. Kościuszki 10, tel: 014 630 03 54.* Situated on the ground floor of the hotel of the same name *(see page 132)*, this combined bar and restaurant retains its original 1970s furniture and decor, including some truly extraordinary sculptured glass. The menu also looks like it was written 30 years ago, but the food is surprisingly good. Worthy of further investigation as a blast-from-the-past experience. Open Mon–Fri 6.30am–midnight, Sat–Sun 7am–midnight.

ZAKOPANE

The natural home of traditional, fatty, meat-heavy Goral-style food, Zakopane has numerous restaurants and outdoor grills serving delicious meat dishes. You'll never go hungry when in town. Many restaurants feature a folk-themed decor, which adds greatly to the atmosphere.

Bąkowo Zohylina $$ *ul. Piłsudskiego 6, tel: 018 201 20 45.* This place serves what's arguably the best local cuisine in town. The meat-heavy menu includes chicken, some excellent shashlik, a lot of pork dishes and something called a Devilish Loin. It's all cooked to perfection, and for once the service hits the mark. The restaurant's rustic setting comes complete with some fine examples of folk art on the walls. Open daily 1pm–midnight.

Gazdowo Kuźnia $$ *ul. Krupówki 1, tel: 018 201 72 01.* Sit in a traditional wooden sleigh and eat vast plates of greasy meat dishes while being served by teenage girls dressed as Heidi. If you're in town during the summer, take advantage of the restaurant's outdoor kebab stall, which sells possibly the best kebabs in Europe. The meat is cut straight from a rotating pig on a spit and served in hot, crispy white bread with lashings of salad and spicy mayonnaise. Open daily 10am–9pm.

Gubałówka $ *ul. Gubałówka, tel: 018 206 36 30.* Among Zakopane's multitude of folk-themed restaurants, this one stands out due to its location at the top of the town's funicular ride. The food is cheap and edible, and its mediocrity is outweighed by the spectacular view of the jagged Tatra Mountains in the distance. Open daily 10am–6pm.

Sphinx $$ *ul. Krupówki 41, tel: 018 206 46 31.* Serving the usual array of spicy meat dishes and plenty of cabbage, this branch of Poland's favourite restaurant chain offers weary tourists sustenance and respite from their excursions into the great Polish outdoors. To complete the picture, there are strings of fairy lights and young waiters in bow ties. Open daily 11am–midnight.

INDEX